Saving the Market from Capitalism

Saving the Market from Capitalism

Ideas for an Alternative Finance

Massimo Amato and Luca Fantacci

Translated by Graham Sells

polity

This volume was originally published in Italy by Donzelli Editore under the title *Come salvare il mercato dal capitalismo* © Donzelli Editore, 2012

This English edition © Polity Press, 2014

Polity Press
65 Bridge Street
Cambridge CB2 1UR, UK

Polity Press
350 Main Street
Malden, MA 02148, USA

ISBN-13: 978-0-7456-7256-4(pb)
ISBN-13: 978-0-7456-7255-7

A catalogue record for this book is available from the British Library.

Typeset in 11 on 13 pt Sabon
by Toppan Best-set Premedia Limited
Printed and bound in Great Britain by T.J. International, Padstow, Cornwall

The publisher has used its best endeavours to ensure that the URLs for external websites referred to in this book are correct and active at the time of going to press. However, the publisher has no responsibility for the websites and can make no guarantee that a site will remain live or that the content is or will remain appropriate.

Every effort has been made to trace all copyright holders, but if any have been inadvertently overlooked the publisher will be pleased to include any necessary credits in any subsequent reprint or edition.

For further information on Polity, visit our website: www.politybooks.com

Contents

Acknowledgements

When working on the ideas that constitute the substance of this book, we enjoyed the benefit of exchanging views with many people to whom we owe thanks.

To begin with, our students, and in particular those who attended with growing involvement, enthusiasm and critical sense the last years of the course in 'History, Institutions and Crisis of the Global Financial System' at the Bocconi University. We must also thank the people who took part in conferences and workshops which we had occasion to attend: it always makes quite an impression to see people of many and varied walks of life who are now compelled willy-nilly to try to get to grips with financial issues, and who are often able to raise questions that are as relevant as they are plain and direct. And again, thanks to Jacopo Tondelli and Jacopo Barigazzi, who dedicated space to our contributions in *Linkiesta*, and to their many readers, always ready with numerous comments: some of the sections assembled here had originally been published in that journal in preliminary versions subsequently modified and completed in the light of the comments. Our gratitude also goes to: Luciano Lanza, who allowed us to republish here an article that previously appeared in *Libertaria*; to Valerio Deambrogio, Lucio Gobbi, Andrea Papetti and Marco Bianchini, with whom we have exchanged views continuously over the last few months; to Luca Larcher, who read the entire manuscript in record time without sparing critical observations; to Jean-Luc Souchet, a leading mutualist and inexhaustible source of advice; to Philippe Mérien and Sandrine Mansour, ever ready to take opportunities for debate and discussion on local currency and, finally, to Abla Bella Banassouh for strong, discreet support.

The errors and oversimplifications that have doubtless found their way into the text are, however, due solely to our stubbornness.

M. A. and L. F.

Introduction

Finance has a crucial role to play, imparting scope and vitality to the economy. Today, however, a form of finance prevails that does not serve this function well: that of financial markets. The dominion of financial markets is politically illegitimate, economically harmful and humanly aberrant. Exit is imperative. And there are already some signs pointing in that direction. This book is intended as a contribution to the conception and design of an alternative finance.*

Despite the crisis, which is above all their crisis, financial markets have achieved unprecedented power. They dictate the law, literally: they impose economic policies, depose governments they find non-compliant, abrogate rights which they see as constraints, sabotage social contracts and reshape the pattern of international equilibria and alliances. So much is a fact. Some also see it as an advantage, a form of discipline, the 'market discipline' that keeps irresponsible governments under the supervision of markets. And some actually see it as a 'virtual senate', the first step towards a global democracy – one dollar, one vote.[1] However, at least until

---

* Massimo Amato is responsible for chapters 1 and 4, and Luca Fantacci for chapters 2 and 3.

we've added to the list of human rights the right to be identified with one's bank account, there are no legitimate foundations for the rule of financial markets. Far from being a new form of democracy, it's a new form of oppression: the dominance of creditors over debtors. In other periods, which we flatter ourselves we have left far behind us, it lay with the political authority to re-balance relations between creditors and debtors. Today, it blithely sanctions the imbalance. We should have learnt the lesson by now, living as we do in countries with limited sovereignty, placed in the charge of their creditors. But perhaps we haven't fully grasped the situation if we are ready to ask China for loans, as if this could really be a way to save Europe.

In a world short of leadership, and even shorter of ideas to manage relations between debtors and creditors, it is the creditors who give the orders to debtors and 'leaders' alike. These, clearly, are the facts, but we cannot accept them as inexorable necessities – we must learn how they have arisen. And this could lead to the discovery that their apparent necessity is in fact open to alternatives. Another form of finance is indeed possible.

Until we've got our ideas straight, there is no point in blaming the creditor at the door, whether it is a German chancellor, a Chinese premier or an international banker. For every creditor is also a debtor. The really novel feature of the new regime that we have to size up is, rather, its impersonal, anonymous and reticular nature, diffuse yet concentrated. True, there are the big banks that make the market and earn a rent, but there are also our pretensions to see some income from our savings recognized as an acquired right – and this is also a form of rent. So here we are, faced with the new 'breed' exercising its authority through the global financial markets; the faceless breed of creditors with no responsibilities. They hold the world in their hands and manage it despotically, demanding sacrifices and handing out rewards.

For some people, this despotism isn't a problem. As they see it, financial markets need no legitimacy other than that deriving from effective performance: financial markets are the optimal instrument for the efficient allocation of resources. If they are a bit cruel, never mind, so long as they work.

The crisis has, however, also brought out a second fact: the financial markets that rule the world do it badly. The dominant finance holds sway over every field of associated life except for the field most directly concerned (just as the dominant economic science claims competence in any question you may raise, precisely, perhaps, to dissimulate its inability to settle purely economic issues). Today, financial markets are doing everything but financing. They play their game, you're told. But it isn't an innocent game, for it can, and today in practice does, prevent others from doing their work. If finance doesn't finance, businesses cannot do business and workers cannot work. Here lies the dissymmetry that the crisis has shown: while finance can grow even without a corresponding growth in the production of commodities and services, the opposite does not hold – the real economy cannot grow without the support of financial services. As the financial markets accomplished their irresistible rise to power, they moved ever further from the economic activities they were supposed to serve.

The crisis has revealed a division between economy and finance, but it did not produce it. If anything, it's just the opposite: it's the division – for years ignored and denied – between economy and finance that brought on first the financial crisis, and then the crisis in the real economy. This is why any efforts to tackle the economic crisis without rethinking the role of financial markets are misguided and doomed to failure.

Freed from its service to the economy, finance has used its power to force its dictates onto governments. However, one thing needs to be made perfectly clear: finance has been able to encroach on the field of politics and subjugate the real economy only because the market ideology has taken over the field of finance. As the fruit of an ideology that no one, in thirty years, has been able to oppose to any effect, the financial market is, as such, a problem. It's an economic, political and, ultimately, human problem. It's a problem because it has taken it upon itself to marketize a basic human and social relationship, that between debtor and creditor. Put like this, the absurdity of the pretension is strikingly obvious. The need, then, is to reform finance in such a way as to drive it back from the area it has encroached upon and restore it to its abandoned task. Depriving finance of its market form means putting it back in the service of the market economy. And this is a political task. Therefore the first, fundamental and overriding priority of political action is to regain its field of freedom and authority and shake off the yoke of ideology.

The 'end of history', proclaimed triumphantly by the neo-liberal doxa on the collapse of the Iron Curtain, was the fruit of a miscalculation. The end of all ideologies was proclaimed, but actually one remained – the ideology of capitalism, in the form of an article of faith attributing the financial markets with all economic rationality. The crisis has shown how ill-founded it was. Even one of its most fervent advocates, Alan Greenspan, had to admit the debacle in a memorable hearing before the US Congress.

It is worth quoting at length the exchanges where Committee Chairman, Senator Waxman, subjected Greenspan to some particularly searching questioning:

> *Chairman Waxman*: The question I have for you is, you had an ideology, you have the belief that free, competitive – and this is your statement – 'I do have an ideology. My judgement is that free, competitive markets are by far the unrivalled way to organise economies. We've tried regulation. None meaningfully worked.' That was your quote. You had the authority to prevent irresponsible lending practices that led to the sub-prime mortgage crisis. You were advised to do so by many others. And now our whole economy is paying its price. Do you feel that your ideology pushed you to make decisions that you wish you had not made?

Greenspan: Well, remember that what an ideology is is a conceptual framework for the way people deal with reality. Everyone has one. You have to – to exist, you need an ideology. The question is whether it is accurate – or not. And what I'm saying to you is, yes, I found a flaw. I don't know how significant or permanent it is, but I've been very distressed by that fact. But if I may, may I just finish an answer to the question...

Chairman Waxman: You found a flaw?...

Greenspan: I found a flaw in the model that I perceived as the critical functioning structure that defines how the world works, so to speak...

Chairman Waxman: In other words, you found that your view of the world, your ideology, was not right, it was not working?

Greenspan: Precisely. That's precisely the reason I was shocked, because I had been going for forty years or more with very considerable evidence that it was working exceptionally well. But just let me, if I may...

Chairman Waxman: Well, the problem is that the time has expired.[2]

It sounds not so much like the 'End of History' so triumphantly announced by Francis Fukuyama as, rather, Samuel Beckett's *Endgame*: the end of a world. But over the last five years we have witnessed a revival of the financial markets, if not of faith in their infallibility. Here lies the paradox of recent times: although the damage they caused is increasingly evident and their usefulness increasingly questionable, financial markets still reign supreme. Indeed, they've actually gained in power. The ideology wobbles but the regime it has helped establish holds out, as is often the case of regimes in decline, with a fierceness goaded through the inability to understand that the game is over. Financial markets persevere in their efforts to dictate the law. And yet, in all honesty, how could any exit from the crisis be thinkable without calling into question one of its deepest causes, which lies precisely in this pretension to dictate the law?

It's time to think about the post-crisis world, and above all to make sure the crisis comes to an end. History shows that crises don't just come to an end unaided, and that the way they end is not always the best of all possible ways. So if we are to exit from the crisis without turning back or, even worse, taking a blind jump, and yet without forgoing the real advantages of globalization, then we must learn to make new distinctions guided by reasonableness rather than ideology.

To begin with, we have to distinguish between markets for actual goods and services, which should be as free, integrated and extensive as possible, and financial markets, which shouldn't even exist.[3] Now, insomuch as capitalism is an economic system historically connoted by the existence of financial markets, a certain distance may, and perhaps should, be taken from capitalism if a truly free market is to be attained. Market economy and capitalism are not synonymous. Actually, they are incompatible. Capitalism is a market economy with one market too many: the money and credit market. Thus some – not nostalgically backward-looking – alternative to the present situation is conceivable.

Why, then, is it so difficult to conceive? What hampers us? What keeps our thoughts from turning to a new contract between state, market and finance? In Keynes's words: the fetish of liquidity. Liquidity is what Keynes, in chapter 12 of *The General Theory*, singled out as the truly distinctive characteristic of financial markets, defining it frankly as an 'anti-social fetish'.[4] Building on this fetish an ideological accord has been established between state and market at the expense of everyone, and above all of society as a whole.

Liquidity is a Janus. On one side, it is the characteristic of credit, in so far as the latter can be bought and sold on a market, namely the financial market, as a place where investments are made without responsibility and everyone stands to gain (a place of 'adolescent freedom', as Mauro Magatti might put it).[5] On the other side, liquidity is also the essential feature of capitalistic money insomuch as it is money that can be held indefinitely as a store of value, as the supreme form of wealth, as a safe refuge in times of uncertainty, when no one can be trusted.

On this twofold fetishist device, a system has been constructed perpetually wavering between the mirage of unconditioned communion and the refuge of absolute solipsism. As long as it worked, it offered the illusion of an artificial paradise of well-being and equality. But when crisis struck all hell broke loose, and the more each sought individual rescue, the more total was the collective debacle.

Throughout all the vicissitudes, however, one principle remained constant: the system sought to turn us all into rentiers. Rent has squeezed wages and profits. The more capital becomes rigid as financial capital, demanding sure returns, the more labour has to be flexible. Hence, the repugnance provoked by the new wealth, as undeserved wealth. Hence also, the increasing disparity in the distribution of wealth, and the inordinate increase in debt to offset the lack of income. And the vicious circle runs round.

Finance has usurped the realm of politics because the market has occupied the terrain of finance. While classical liberalism defended the market from politics and social democracy defended politics from the market, no one has troubled to defend finance from the market, or the market economy from capitalism.

And yet it deserves to be avowed: the essence of finance is social. It has to do with the relationship between debtor and creditor. Questioning the way financial markets work does not, therefore, mean authorizing out-of-hand demonization of the banks and stock exchanges. Psychologically understandable as it may be in times of social distress, this is no way to get down to the causes, nor to determine where all the blame lies. It's an approach that looks no further than for scapegoats. It may be unpopular to say so, but it must be said plainly and simply: the blame does not lie with 'someone else', for we are all part of the financial markets in so far as we share, socially and individually, the anti-social assumptions they run on. We are all involved in this odious regime of creditors. To start with, we are all creditors: the simple fact of having a bank account means helping build up on the debtor a pressure that can become unendurable. Above all, however, and at a more basic level, even people who don't invest in stocks and bonds, and possibly protest against the excessive power of Wall Street, are still hardly likely to call into question the underlying principle of the financial markets – the dogma of liquidity. This consists in the apparently natural idea that cash (liquidity, in other words) is the safest form of saving and, consequently, one will part with it only for an investment that is equally liquid or that yields sufficient interest to compensate for the lack of liquidity. This, in short, is the general creed we all respect: money is the supreme good, and must generate interest when it is lent. If you accumulate money, you expect it to retain its value. If you loan it, you expect to get a bit more back. A dollar tomorrow is worth less than a dollar today: you take this for granted, you count on it, you quite literally discount it. Thus operates the dogma of the liquid trinity: money–credit–interest, three in one, inseparable. Who would question this dogma nowadays? And yet it is precisely upon this undisputed assumption that the power of financial markets rests: the by now proverbial greed of bankers and dealers on the stock exchange would be powerless and harmless if they didn't have this mighty lever to work with.

But there is still more to it. Independently of the financial markets, the idea that money is wealth and that the mere lending of it merits a reward is the root of an endemic evil that is both social and human. Call it as you will. Until a couple of centuries ago, it was called usury. Then the classical economists called it rent, and criticized it harshly. Today it's called rate of interest. In any case, it is income obtained without working or running entrepreneurial risks and is thus quite distinct from both the worker's wage and the entrepreneur's profit.

Now, it may seem trite to point it out, but in times like these we'd better try to be basic: if somewhere someone is making money without working, somewhere else someone is working without making money. That is why economic rent is structurally intolerable. It is, in Aristotle's word, hateful – whether concentrated in the hands of a few rentiers or distributed 'democratically' to all. To start with, it's hateful to the people who pay it, which means every one of us as a debtor, for it constitutes a forced levy, a tax, and one that can become an unbearable burden to the extent of having the effect of political and economic blackmail (as Alan Greenspan once pointed out, 'an American in debt is an American who can't afford to go on strike'). More generally speaking, it's hateful to society as a whole, for it accentuates disparities in income distribution and continually saps lymph from the vital parts of the economic system, from labour and firms, feeding sterile accumulation. Finally, it is hateful to those who receive it, in other words every one of us as creditors, for it lulls us all into the illusion that one can live without working, without running risks and even without desiring anything definite apart from money, to the extent of sacrificing everything else to it, in the self-destructive obsession to liquidate everything – the modern-day version of the curse of Midas.

The indignation of protesters over the last few months demonstrating for 'less speculation, more imagination' is perfectly understandable, and in fact we understand it. But indignation is not enough. If we want to take a real distance from the present financial system, then we must start thinking up an alternative system that is also feasible; for one important fact remains, and there can be no getting away from it: if economic life has no need of the stock exchanges as we know them, people nevertheless have the vital need to give and receive credit. We could do perfectly well without financial markets, but we can't do without finance. Essentially, finance is the space of the relationship between debtor and creditor; a space where someone can give credit to a promise (promissory note) since whoever makes that promise has a responsibility to honour it (by paying), and where both, jointly responsible, have to face the risk that, for some unforeseeable eventuality, regardless of their intentions, payment may be jeopardized and may need to be renegotiated. Where this space is open, the economy can breathe and there is scant risk that, simply for lack of money, a deal is not brought off, a person does not work or a new productive enterprise fails to take off.

Saying no to financial markets does not mean forgoing finance. Indeed, a constructive 'no' could at last imply a form of finance adequate to its task. On financial markets, a debt is a negotiable security; in the other finance, a debt is an obligation to be honoured. On financial markets, the settling of accounts is constantly postponed, unless it looms up unexpectedly in a crisis; in the other finance, debtor and creditor concur in making possible the settlement of each account as it comes up. Financial markets are based on liquidity; the other finance is founded on responsibility. On financial markets, there is competition to place or withdraw funds; in the other finance, there is cooperation to make advance and settlement possible. On financial markets, risk is systemic and crisis endemic; in the other finance, a firm may fail but the system won't.

Finally, saying no to financial markets certainly doesn't mean forgoing the market. It simply means refraining from putting on the market something that is not a commodity, namely money and credit. It means having at last for true commodities a market where demand and supply meet without distortions. The wild fluctuations in the prices of raw materials that we have witnessed with the crisis show just how much financial markets can interfere with the functioning of commodity markets. Some limits must be set to markets for money and credit if we want free competitive markets for actual goods and services, appropriately regulated and delimited, able to preserve the freedom upon which they are based.

Setting limits to the market is a political task. Where is the line to be drawn? Between true commodities and fictitious commodities, beginning with credit, which is not a commodity but a relationship. If the market extends to credit, there's no holding the floodwater back – sooner or later it will bring the dams down. Either we start subtracting credit from the market, or regulation and, moreover, democratization of globalization is just wishful thinking.

What does it mean to set limits to the market for money and credit? Some measures have already been mooted and only need to be implemented within an organic framework: they can take the form of a financial transactions tax, increased taxation on financial returns, inheritance and wealth taxes, regulatory distinction between commercial and investment banks.

However, limiting financial markets is not the only goal worth pursuing. It is also possible, and indeed desirable, to invent new forms. Thinking about an alternative means putting one's mind to another kind of finance, moving on from market finance to finance for the market.

Finance has two essential tasks to perform: funding trade and financing investments. Neither of these tasks requires a market for credit or interest-bearing loans. Funding trade can be achieved through clearing systems (characterized not by indefinite growth in financial operations but by equilibrium in trade). Investments and innovation can be financed through forms of profit-and-loss sharing (in which growth is not obligatory but simply possible). With both these financial forms, it is possible to keep finance closely bound up with real economic activity. Both are forms of cooperative finance.

Delimiting and reforming finance are urgent political undertakings. At stake is not only the health of the economic system but the restoration and preservation of breathing space for the political system and democracy itself. Reform of finance can and must be achieved at all levels: international, European, national and local. It can also start from the bottom, in keeping with a principle of subsidiarity and in the spirit of our best cooperative tradition. Europe itself needs to find new forms of cooperation, in particular through a clearing house to settle all the imbalances that have accumulated over the last ten years. Here, the model could be the European Payments Union (EPU), which enabled post-war recovery, as well as the Italian and German economic miracles of the 1950s. Local experiments are starting up throughout Europe, not to counter the euro but to reinforce monetary union. Similar initiatives are starting to flourish also in Italy. And it would be nice to see Italy, having now regained a credible say in European affairs, promote a renewal – in finance in particular – as it has done in the most glorious moments of its past.

In the spirit of our previous publications, the idea behind this book is to contribute to opening a new area of debate and keeping it open – not to offer dogmatically conceived prescriptions against the tired old dogmas of neoliberalism.

The first step to take on the way out of crisis must be to escape from the lure of doctrinaire formulas. The neoliberal dogmas and the partisan propaganda that they have generated over the last thirty years hide a basic weakness: the 'principle' they elevate to dogma – liquidity – is in reality no principle but an illusion, a trap.

Exit from the – primarily ideological – crisis of the last few years calls for identification of a principle upon which to construct new forms of finance, and towards which to guide back certain forms of finance already there but hitherto marginalized. Starting from the evidence of a finance for the market, as opposed to a market finance, it will be possible to single out step by step the specific tools to be refined, and to identify the various levels at which we must learn to apply them.

What is already apparent, if only we open our eyes, is that the other finance we refer to – not a market finance but a finance for the market – is no utopia. It is possible to save the market from capitalism, and economic science from ideology. There are numerous examples, ancient and modern, of a finance that has no need of financial markets, from the exchange fairs of the Renaissance to the new forms of corporate barter; from the traditional cooperative banks to more recent systems of local exchange. And there are a great many ancient and modern examples of finance not entailing interest-bearing loans, from Islamic finance to venture capital, from the experiments with stamp scrip during the Great Depression to certain present-day forms of complementary currency. New proposals are also finding circulation for reform of the international monetary system, and even for the institution of a European clearing system. Gathering such seeds of innovation, our aim with this book is to contribute to the conception, design and promotion of a different, cooperative finance, seen not as a market but as the space for the relationship between debtor and creditor.

1

Why Can We Find No Exit from the Crisis?

Of all the reforms being considered to avert the crisis, in Italy, as indeed elsewhere, why is reform of the financial system no longer on the agenda? Why is the idea setting in that the only way out of the crisis lies in the fiscal consolidation of states, seen in turn as a necessary condition to relaunch growth?

The only explanation lies in a hypothesis that waxes all the stronger the less the need is felt to explain it, namely the idea that it is necessary and indeed desirable to get back into working order that system of relations between finance and real economy which is at the origin of the crisis that broke out in 2007 and is still taking its toll, calling on the real economy to take upon itself the entire burden of adjustment.

Be that as it may. But why, if the sole aim is to return to the old status quo, is this conservative programme so insistently placed under the heading of 'reforms'? Why this insistence on denying that the crisis has called into question the institutional–ideological model of relations between economy and finance underlying the financial globalization of the last thirty years? Why does the conviction still hold that there are no practicable alternatives to the financial system as we know it? Why is all the talk spent on passing off conservation of a system for reform not being exposed for what it really is, a purely rhetorical apparatus?

There's no getting away from it. The first condition for tackling the problem is not to deny it. The second is to see it for what it is, and there is nothing like fear to blind one to a realistic view of the situation.

So how do we overcome fear? In his famous inaugural address, Roosevelt said that 'the only thing we have to fear is fear itself.' So far so good, but how do we turn a fine-sounding formula into a plan of action? A tale with a Zen accent goes, 'One day fear knocked on the door. Hope went to open it. There was no longer anybody there.' Fine, but where can we place our hopes if they are not to prove as misleading as our fears?

Woody Allen, a humorist who can come up with flashes of extraordinary wisdom, had something to say about hope that was much more than a paradox and that, after some initial bewilderment, could prove truly helpful: 'More than any time in history, mankind faces a crossroads. One path leads to despair and utter hopelessness, the other to total extinction. Let us pray that we have the wisdom to choose correctly.'

The first point here lies in recognizing that despair is not necessarily a passive and negative state, above all when it's the only alternative to extinction. Literally, despair can be the state of those who have given up hoping, but not acting. Rhetoric aside, faced with the evermore imminent risk of the collapse of a system of relations between economy and finance that we are accustomed to consider as having no alternative, we must keep as cool and collected as we can. Instead of relying on hopes that are as misplaced as the fears they are supposed to dispel, we should simply size up the present situation with the analytical tools and energy that we effectively have.

Keynes defined the urge to action, characterizing enterprise with a much misconstrued expression: animal spirits. What are we to make of 'animal spirits' if not unfoundedly optimistic or even irrational excitement? If fear can easily lead to unreasonable choices, optimism and unchecked will-power are no less dangerous. So how are we to take this expression, which certainly does not mean 'animal impulses'?

There's a passage in *The General Theory* that sets us on the right road. Keynes writes:

> It is safe to say that enterprise which depends on hopes stretching into the future benefits the community as a whole. But individual initiative will only be adequate when reasonable calculation is supplemented and supported by animal spirits, so that the thought of ultimate loss which often overtakes pioneers, as experience undoubtedly tells us and them, is put aside as a healthy man puts aside the expectation of death.[1]

Far from being opposed to calculation and dispassionate analysis of the situation, animal spirits complement calculation and enable action in conditions of uncertainty. Every enterprise needs reason and courage or, better, rationality reasonably tempered by the capacity to 'stick to its guns', even when explanations are lacking and calculation does not offer sufficient grounds for decisions that cannot be deferred. The very uncertain task which the crisis is driving us to undertake, at all levels, is nothing short of a radical reform of finance and, above all, of its relations with the real economy. Can we even begin to adumbrate the combination of calculation and courage, science and sangfroid necessary to carry it through?

We have already quoted Roosevelt. That the situation today is no sunnier than that of the 1930s is by now evident to many. Several governments throughout Europe have declared the intention to discuss anew the stability pact so as to 'combine rigour with growth'. At the same time, as the old equilibria fall away, the more or less openly 'self-centred', not to say nationalistic, positions show a certain inclination to give way to cooperative attitudes. Let's hope so. However, when we hear it repeated that the time has come to combine rigour with growth, we must ask ourselves, as a matter of intellectual honesty, what 'combine' means in this context. Alongside growth in production and income there must be a reset of finance. The reset of finance must not get in the way of growth in production and income, of course. But how are we to move on from proclamations to action?

Paul Valéry coined an aphorism that has enjoyed a fair circulation: with the labels on bottles, we can neither get drunk nor quench our thirst. Precisely because it's a serious issue, and the thirst for reform is real, we mustn't stop short at the labels, but we must also avoid getting drunk. Rigour and sobriety are two different things, as indeed are recklessness and courage.

And then, in the first place, it's a matter of being able to read, even if only labels. The history of finance reminds us that there exists a financial rigour that thwarts growth and indeed fosters depression, but it also tells us that there is a way to finance growth generating euphoria, which serves only to open the way to more and worse crises. Scylla and Charybdis loom ahead, and we must learn to sail, keeping a distance from both monsters, or in other words finding a middle way. The 'happy medium', however, is not a petit bourgeois virtue, nor the refuge of the mediocre: by virtue of it, Ulysses found a way out using his shrewdness, not turning his back on the two opposed perils threatening him, but succeeding in finding equidistance from both. The middle way calls for a spirit of innovation, courage and intelligence.

Combining rigour and growth means establishing healthy relations between finance and real economy. Up until 2007, growth was enabled by the systematic accumulation of financial imbalances; when they exploded in the form of private defaults, losses were socialized through public intervention, and the sovereign debt crisis now experienced set in. The rigour being called for to re-balance the public accounts only leads us ever further from any chances of organizing recovery. On the other hand, as long as we keep trying to stimulate growth through injections of liquidity, the 'remedy' only makes matters worse in an endless spiral that brings the economies even further under the blackmail of financial markets. Similar attempts to overcome the crisis generated by finance enhance the power of financial markets to exert pressure.

The relationship between finance and real economy seems to have been totally inverted, which is why it is in the first place precisely upon this relationship that intervention must concentrate. And the road to take, that middle road, is in the direction of reform of the financial institutions, founding them on a principle very different from the one they have been so precariously made to rest upon in the last thirty years, not to say the last three centuries. What this principle is and what alternative there may be will be considered in the following pages.

The End of Liquidity Finance

Alarming as it may be to admit it, there can be no getting away from the fact: since the year 2007, the world has been in a state of crisis from which there's no turning back. The deluge is not 'after us'. All that was to happen has happened, what was to finish is over and there is no *belle époque* to return to. In precisely what sense, we will see at greater length later on. For now, suffice it to look back to a conclusion we drew in a book written five years ago, which, alas, required no changes for the second edition brought out a few years later. We would have preferred otherwise, but nothing new has happened in terms of the reforms contemplated and urged there.[2]

The conclusion runs as follows: what began in 2007 as a liquidity crisis of the financial markets rapidly turned out to be a crisis of liquidity as the basis of market finance. If, then, the crisis is at the level of principles, it is at this level that the solutions are to be sought. All the rest are mere expedients to plug a hole in a dam doomed to collapse. Like the plucky little Dutch boy in the story, the ruling classes that had emerged before the crisis set about cramming their fingers into the crack opening in the dam. But, behind the dam, ever stormier billows have been piling up. The dam has been patched up, but the floodwaters are near to overflowing.

The metaphor of the dam and the floodwaters is in fact all too appropriate. From the year 2007 onwards, the liquidity crisis of the markets and financial institutions has been addressed with massive injections of liquidity, which have allowed the financing of growing sovereign debts. They have been necessary and perhaps (let's hope not) insufficient to prevent a debacle for a number of European countries and the single currency. At the same time, they risk feeding inflationary pressures, encouraging irresponsible borrowing and paving the way to further crises. Yet it is hardly surprising that these are the effects when the idea is to plug a hole in a dam – with injections of liquidity!

What exactly is meant by 'liquidity'? In short, it is the principle in virtue of which debts are made not to be paid but to be bought and sold on that *sui generis* market which is the financial market. Liquidity transforms the risk inherent to every act of credit, namely the risk that the debtor may not be able to pay, into a very different risk: the risk that the securities representing the debts find no purchasers. Liquidity transforms credit risk into liquidity risk.[3]

As long as there are purchasers, no debt is excessive for, in principle, a potentially insolvent debtor will always be able to cover the debts by issuing more securities. Insolvency emerges when the market no longer absorbs the new issues. The point is, however, that it emerges – it isn't that it comes about at that moment. We'll go into the more technical aspect in the second part of this book, but it's just as well to make it clear from the start: the debts that eventually proved to be unpayable, like the Greek debt, were already so from the outset, when the financing of them began without any precautions. The crisis broke out when these ever unpayable debts also became unsaleable. Continuing with our example, what played a crucial role in the accumulation of crisis conditions for the Greek sovereign debt was never cool and rigorous technical analysis of the state of health of the Greek economy, or indeed of the way the Greeks spent the money that they were lent. If thinking had run along these lines at the time, we wouldn't be in such a sorry plight today. The crucial role was, however, played by expectations regarding the liquidity of the securities representing that debt. As long as all were ready to buy them, the returns and consequently the spread in relation to other, more solid securities remained low. But no rate of interest is high enough to prevent an honest and earnest speculator in the North from betting on Greek default, or in other words selling Greek securities, thereby making financing ever more difficult and default ever more probable. What a pleasure it is to go on doing the right thing, first buying blindly and then selling equally blindly!

There are no good guys nor villains. It may well be that Greece is a country which, through its own fault, can no longer service its debt, if indeed it is not an insolvent country. Insolvent or not, the fact remains that its crisis is a liquidity crisis – and, as such, risks spreading with no limits or defences. This is why it's time for everyone to stop being always right and start being a bit more reasonable.

Liquidity crises come about in a finance that sets liquidity as its principle, and injections of liquidity do not settle them. In fact, they only generate the sort of situation we have been experiencing for some months, and which Japan has known for twenty years: a liquidity trap, or in other words a situation in which no increase in the overall liquidity of the system, no creation of money, can induce the recipients to use it, putting it into circulation. The banks and the various other agencies keep the cash well stowed away. And this accounts for, on the one hand, the failure of the European Central Bank's (ECB) recent ambitious financial measures, lending about a thousand billion euros to European banks, which promptly deposited them in the ECB, and, on the other hand, the credit squeeze or, better, credit crunch besetting firms, which find ever less credit coming their way.

At this point, we come back to the issue of the relations between finance and real economy. We now find ourselves in the paradoxical situation in which the financial markets and agents have for some time got back to work, reaping profits, distributing bonuses and dictating agendas to the governments, although the real depression only gets worse. However, we cannot in all good faith simply fall back on blaming the 'greed' of the 'speculators'. The evil is not so much a moral as an 'architectural' problem. Reproachable individual behaviours are always possible. Indeed, over the last few years, the financial world has come up with some brilliant examples. But surely it's time we recognized the fact that all the individual misdeeds are dwarfed by the major problem: the very relations between finance and economy are ill-founded. 'I'm not bad, I'm just drawn that way,' said a cartoon lady in a film a few years ago. How much longer must we wait to realize that the crucial flaw lies in the design of the system, indeed in its very principle? Or, to be even more precise, it lies in the fact that the principle is a pseudo-principle? If we did, we could then realize that things stood just the same way before the crisis, and that there is nothing worth going back to.

For here lies the rhetorical self-deception that is now being passed off as sound common sense: we've exaggerated, we've spent more than we could afford and now it's time to 'tighten our belts', to toe the line alongside the virtuous. The latter, in the meantime, have been looking on, urging us reproachfully to get a move on and follow their example. Once we have all re-assumed a serious stance, we can start growing again.

Instead of complaining, why don't we ask ourselves the simple question: how is it that some have been able to afford what they couldn't afford? The answer is of a dumbfounding simplicity: before the crisis, this very same system which now denies everyone everything with unrelenting severity had denied nobody anything. The virtuous creditors who now claim the right to look on reproachfully and disapprovingly had played the role of blinkered financial backers to the very people now seen as sinners to be redeemed by forcing on them stupidly penitential procedures, with a touch of sadism.

Didn't the people who financed Greece realize what they were doing? Were they misguided or Mephistophelian?

Actually, they were neither: they simply acted, like everyone, in a situation where nobody was held responsible. In a system based on liquidity, there is absolutely no need for the creditors to enquire with due diligence about the real solvency conditions of their debtors, at least as long as the market is ready to absorb at all times and at a good price as many securities as, having created them, they subsequently wish to shed.

'I seem to be dreaming,' says a Lehman executive in the film *Margin Call* on realizing that his bank is stuffed with securities that should rightly be defined by a four-letter word (the great chief paraphrases with 'stinking excrement'). 'No, you've just woken up,' promptly answers a cynical colleague, appropriately but perhaps not all that wittingly. Actually, the only realization that could prevent all of us – financiers and politicians, citizens and savers, economists and millenarists – from falling asleep again would consist in recognizing that the name of the sleeping drug we have all been making excessive use of is liquidity. Heraclitus said that when men are awake, they live in a world common to all, but when they are asleep, each is in his own 'world'. All the better for him, we seem to have thought. And we have attempted to construct an 'economic world' where all we have in common is precisely the somnambulism induced by liquidity.

To call it a gross error is putting it mildly. But what made it possible? We can hardly blame greed, which is a vice of the wakeful. It is in fact a far more common need, unfortunately even better distributed than the good sense of Descartes – the need for reassurance. Once again, Keynes put it aptly: 'The desire to hold money as a store of wealth is a barometer of the degree of our distrust of our own calculations and conventions concerning the future.... The possession of actual money lulls our disquietude; and the premium we require to make us part with money is a measure of the degree of our disquietude.'[4]

This need for reassurance is inversely proportional to the capacity to face the risk inherent in every economic activity. Left to one's own devices, there is a natural tendency to shirk responsibilities and fall back on 'that's what everyone does'. You need not be bad to do wrong; it's enough to let yourself go. Hence, anthropologically, the need for Law. But what if the law itself authorizes shirking all responsibility? In the financial world, an unwritten law has sanctioned the right to be irresponsible for creditors and debtors alike, albeit in different forms, giving rise to the construction of a gigantic reassurance mechanism that has made liquidity its tool and its principle.

Yet, if the principle is unfounded, no tool really works. And authentic, radical reform – the only reform that will do – cannot in this case start from the tools; it must start from the principle. The solution to this epochal crisis can be sought and eventually found only if we start at the level of principles. The liquidity principle is a false principle, a principle that does not hold. Why doesn't it? The fact is, it is based on the destruction – the annihilation – of the fundamental relationship in every economic system, and in particular, again as Keynes observed, that upon which every true market economy rests: the relationship between debtors and creditors.

The Good Old Days Were Already Bad

Gains for all at zero risk: ultimately, this is what the liquidity system meant – the dream of the rentier, well represented by the comfortably sprawling saver in a TV commercial boasting of the heaps of money he's making to the panting cyclists passing by (on their way to work, poor fools!).

But if he's making money reclined, who are the others fruitlessly on their feet? For someone's got to do the work, out of sight in some cellar, perhaps, hidden from the taxman. In Buñuel's film *The Phantom of Liberty*, the roles are reversed: odious behaviour is publicly boasted while work figures as a cost to be kept to a minimum, if anything at all – and not as the only legitimate source of legitimate gains.

Until crisis broke out, financial rents, and with them the financial markets that generate them, could pass off as socially acceptable because the financial markets not only generated returns but brought money flowing into all the pockets, of firms and consumers alike, without any particular discriminatory criteria.

'Teach everyone everything' (*omnes omnia omnino*) was the motto of a pioneer of modern pedagogy, Comenius. Words are a common commodity, and knowledge too. That none be denied knowledge is the principle of any society meant to be effectively democratic. Words are a universal right.

In some respects, money is like words. The point is, in which respects? When it's a matter of the given word, the promise which establishes the relationship between debtor and creditor, the creditor has the duty – also in the interests of the debtor – not to grant more credit than the debtor is likely to be able to pay back when the appointed time comes. But giving anyone all they ask has become the sole financial pedagogy deliberately practised over the last thirty years to make finance 'democratic'.

The democratization of finance has become the fig leaf hiding the financialization of the economy – and of democracy. It doesn't take a hidebound Marxist to see that many posts in governments are occupied by men and women who come from the big banks – and who sometimes even go back to them.

With the present crisis, this pedagogy has revealed its profound asociality. The nightmare situation now enveloping the economy is the exact reverse of the dream that held us lulled until 2007. The financial imperative now reigning is the exact reverse of the previous version: don't lend anyone anything is the only rule that can be respected when liquidity crisis turns into liquidity trap. Ultimately, however, it simply reflects with mathematical precision the corresponding shortcomings in education and consequent sense of sociality.

Basically, what people fail to see in the first place is that finance was in crisis even before the crisis of the financial markets, and precisely because it was a finance based on financial markets. In fact, these markets thrive on the destruction of the fundamental element in all economic sociality: the relationship between debtor and creditor.

We have made the point over and over again, but perhaps it still needs some repeating. The relationship between debtors and creditors is as necessary as it is hazardous: necessary because there is no actor in the real economy who has no need of advances, and thus of finance, to be able to act; dangerous, because the promise to pay the debt associated with the granting of credit is, precisely, a promise, and no one can know with certainty whether it will be possible for it to be honoured. The creditor does not know, nor indeed does the debtor. Hence the need for careful evaluation and, by extension, for financial intermediaries. The role of the banker is not to sell more or less remunerative or structured financial products, but to make professional evaluation of the would-be debtors' creditworthiness, able also to take risks at the right moment with the support of their own resources. For not even bankers are omniscient: no economic agent can elude what Keynes called 'fundamental uncertainty'.

Uncertainty is fundamental in the sense that it underlies every economic act, simply because economic action is performed in the temporal dimension and each economic calculation and act entails evaluation of future events. Some are foreseeable, in the sense that we can at least attribute to them a certain probability. Others aren't.

Ideally taking a modern, secular and unprejudiced perspective on the world, we are obsessed with the need for certainty, perhaps in part because we shy away from the one certainty we all have, and which should teach us something: the certainty of our death. Certain as a fact, the death of each of us is for each uncertain in terms of the exact moment. Otherwise our lives would be something like life on death row, knowing the date of the sentence well in advance. Living means reckoning with the unforeseeability of the future, which is as vital as it is, possibly, distressing. In general, to start with and most of the time, we make no resort to the support of our animal spirits to face up to uncertainty: rather, we turn our back on it, seeking assurance and reassurance without always being over-subtle in our search. No harm in this, as it goes, unless – as may happen – the pursuit of assurance takes the upper hand, generating an absolute need for absolute certainty. When the need for certainty becomes absolute, we lose contact with reality and become potential prey to all sorts of illusions. The worst of these is the self-delusion that we can calculate every risk and so guard against it.

We are not 'philosophizing' here and taking a break from economics. Precisely because we mean to deal with economics and not one of its ideological surrogates, we cannot avoid some essential questions. We must inquire into the metaphysical origins of the liquidity dogma and of the derivative products accompanying the attempt to impose it as the very principle of finance, or rather of the financialization of the economy. Let us try to explain.

Perhaps not all risks can be avoided, but we can guard against their effects, and in particular against their economic effects. The risk of my debtor's bankruptcy is less daunting if I can insure myself against its effects. True enough; and if whoever insures me against this risk can in turn free himself of the risk by selling it to others ready to buy it on sufficiently extensive markets, then I may well take it that the overall risk is not so much reduced as, rather, distributed in a balanced way. But when this progressive extension loses any association with limits, to become an endless chain reaction, it's a different state of affairs: legitimate interest in keeping danger away becomes the daydream of getting rid of risk by commercializing it. This brings us to the point made at the beginning of this chapter and the implicit assumption behind liquidity finance: if no one is to take responsibility for the risk run, then everyone risks and everyone stands to gain more.

As long as it lasts.

Then we find we no longer want to risk any more, and we suddenly realize that no one deserves our confidence, and that even sovereign states are worth ever less financially

– eventually about as much as a beggar in the eyes of the proverbial 'Bradford millionaire'.

The problem, however, that arises when you no longer trust others is that there's no point in seeking relations with anyone else on an equal footing. Partners become potential adversaries, not because they compete with us but because we can't trust them as partners. The trouble is that trade and the economy in general need trust in order to prosper. If, far from supporting confidence, finance aims at doing without it, then the going gets really hard.

The Principle of an Alternative Finance

Here we come to the point. The market economy does not rest upon competition, but on cooperation, given the simple fact that every real economy is founded on the debtor–creditor relationship.

Necessary yet hazardous, the debtor–creditor relationship entails the need for assurance. It's perfectly natural to seek it, precisely because the relationship is indeed essential. But it's pure folly to seek it at the cost of ruining the relationship.

This, and nothing more, is the sense of the financial markets founded on liquidity, which springs from the severing of the relationship between debtors and creditors that lies in transforming the relationship into a commodity, a piece of paper, bought and sold on the basis of monetizing the risk inherent in its sale. The risk is no longer a credit risk, associated with the fundamental uncertainty about the future of the real investment that occasioned the tying of the debt relationship, but a liquidity risk, associated with the degree of probability that the holders of the securities will be able to readily sell them whenever they like.

The year 2007 saw the emergence of unpayable debts, not in the sense that hitherto all debts had been payable and all the debtors were solvent, as the rating agencies had given us to understand. The fact that the debts accumulated before 2007 could not be paid was not seen as a problem thanks only to the illusion of liquidity; when they were eventually seen to be unpayable, they became unbuyable, and so unsaleable. Again, before 2007 all debts were saleable, whether payable or not, and there was credit for everyone. After 2007, all debts, both payable and unpayable alike, were no longer buyable, and there was no more credit for anyone.

Guarding against a risk that is heavy but bearable by creating another that seems relatively slight, only to become suddenly unmanageable, is not, one would think, a particularly intelligent ploy. And yet there is an intelligent way to ward off risk which is just as old as, if not older than, the way devised by the financial markets. The right approach to a risk that weighs on a relationship is not individual flight, hoping to pass it off on someone else, like the queen of spades in the card game called 'Old Maid': whoever's left holding the ill-omened lady in the end is the loser. A risk that is born and dies away with the relationship that generates it is minimized by bearing it together. The economically appropriate response to the risk inherent to credit is cooperation – cooperation between debtors and creditors.

So, do we go on from philosophizing to moralizing? Are we preaching universal love between enemies? Are we making assumptions that are in contrast with 'true human nature', which is obviously a selfish, bestial nature? Rest assured, we are not. We are sticking to the field of economics, or rather, perhaps, getting right into it now.

There is finance and finance, and not all forms of finance are equal. Even though the 'human material' remains the same; even though we are all capable of turning into rampaging imbeciles without, normally, much effort, for it is usually enough just to let oneself go; even though no practicable institutional reform can entail as a condition the final transformation of human nature (there would, perhaps, be no need of institutions if we were all good); even if we are indeed stuck with these realities, the fact remains that there are some situations that encourage, and others that discourage, the human tendency to act against self and others.

Is there such a thing as a finance so conceived as to be concretely, and not just theoretically, in the service of the economy? A finance adequate to the uncertainties that inevitably surround every economic action and every calculation? As colleagues of the author of a slim but successful volume on *The Basic Laws of Human Stupidity*, and above all as readers of chapter 24 of Keynes's *General Theory*, we are not dreaming of 'moral revolution' or, worse, the abolition of imbecility (*vaste programme*, as de Gaulle would have said). We are simply seeking to bring readers to the fundamentals of a finance for the market, as opposed to the current market finance.

These fundamentals include the principle of symmetrical obligations. There is, obviously, an obligation on the part of the debtor: the debt must be paid. But there is also a responsibility for the creditor, which consists in following lines of economic behaviour so as to make it possible for debtors as a whole to pay their debts. The imbalance in accounts constituted by the debt of the debtor is matched by another imbalance represented by the credit of the creditor: the only balance imaginable in accounting terms is one in which the debts offset the credits and vice versa. Otherwise, we would be in the terminological quandary of having to imagine something even more balanced than balance itself. There is debt, which is imbalance, and there is balance, which is a matter of having no debts, and then there is the matter of having credit, which is – what?

Until some economist-turned-alchemist comes along, able to transform the credit position into a position that can be taken on by all economic agents at the same time (or, simply, until we can flood the Martian markets with our exports), we prefer to think that the creditor has an obligation symmetrical (which does not, mind you, mean equal) to that of the debtor.

The debtor has to pay. It's as simple as it is honest. The creditor has to spend. Both, paying and spending, are uses proper to money, but they are different uses, which we must not confuse. In practice, indeed, we can only confuse them if we treat money as a commodity, and as a form of wealth.

Sell and Let Sell

To remind us that money accumulated, even in consequence of sale or saving, is not wealth, there is not only the myth of Midas, and not only all the criticism of the gold fetishism characterizing mercantilism, according to the liberal economists including, most notably, Smith. Much closer to us, we also have the historical examples of the Marshall Plan and the European Payments Union.

Actually, we know what it was that prompted General Marshall, who was not an economist but US army chief of staff during the Second World War, to propose when secretary of state in 1947 the plan that bears his name. The United States emerged from the war with a net credit position vis-à-vis the rest of the world, an expanding economy and a huge export capacity while on the other side of the Atlantic it had starving partners with empty coffers. It's their fault, and so their business, the Americans might have said after the Second World War, as indeed they had after the First. However, once in a while the lessons of history are absorbed, and sometimes the generals get there before the economists. Marshall brought Congress round to non-repayable funding for the reconstruction of Europe, not out of the goodness of his heart, but because, as he put it, in this way the United States was in the first place doing itself a favour.

And, once in a while, there are even some economists who have good advice to give, too. In another context, and a few years earlier, Keynes put the point the general was to make, but with greater precision and style:

> A country finding itself in a creditor position against the rest of the world as a whole should enter into an obligation to dispose of this credit balance and not to allow it meanwhile to exercise a contractionist pressure against the world economy and, by repercussion, against the economy of the creditor country itself. This would give us, and all others,

the great assistance of multilateral clearing. [...] This is not a Red Cross philanthropic relief scheme, by which the rich countries come to the rescue of the poor. It is a piece of highly necessary business mechanism, which is at least as useful to the creditor as to the debtor.[5]

One can't help wondering why it is so difficult to see that we are in the same situation in Europe today and that, quite simply, there are other countries in the role of the United States and defeated Germany, but the logic remains the same. Even more, we can only wonder why the similarity is so difficult to grasp, given that Europe was constructed by also taking Keynes's advice into account. Passed over at Bretton Woods in 1944 to die in 1946, Keynes became the ideal moving spirit behind the EPU which functioned, between 1950 and 1958, as a multilateral clearing house for the payment of commercial transactions between European countries. Thanks to the EPU, the needy countries of Europe could import from other countries with no restrictions save the capacity to export after having imported, while the European countries able to export could do so without the liquidity shortages of their potential clients stopping the latter from purchasing. Under only one condition: the creditor countries must spend their credits within the clearing circuit. The result was even more miraculous than the undeniably brilliant outcomes of the Marshall Plan. In the 1950s, Europe saw extremely high average growth rates and became a peaceful interconnected market, as well as a partner, and subsequently a formidable competitor, for the United States.

What remains to be seen, in keeping with Keynes's rationale, is the extent to which it is not a matter of non-repayable humanitarianism but rather of sound economy, and indeed to what extent the economy thus delineated proves worthy of the human beings that apply it or of the prestige or interests of the countries that trade brings together.

We'll start from the end: it is an economy useful to debtor and creditor alike because it reduces at the same time both the debtor's risk of not being able to pay and the creditor's risk of not being paid. This is achieved by virtue of the fact that the creditors spend, avoiding the build-up of contractionist pressure which would eventually hit them too.

It's fairly straightforward: to be creditors means having been sellers, and being sellers means having found buyers. It's thanks to the buyers that there can be creditors: the creditor owes his position to the buyer, and can pay his debt only through the practice of reciprocity by buying in turn. Otherwise, the game breaks off, the debtors go bankrupt and the creditors stop selling. *Mors tua, mors mea.* So, sell and let sell...

The Keynesian solution is more intelligent and economical than the Marshallian one (in the sense of Marshall the general, of course, not the economist) because it is multilateral and cooperative whereas the other is bilateral and potentially unbalanced. Behind Marshall's gifts is the donor's tendency, not too well concealed, to consider himself morally in credit with the donee; Keynes's self-interested obligation rests on the recognition of an essential equality amongst all the actors without moral implications.

Today, however, the tendency is to explain economic issues with moral attitudes. It is precisely this that we, as economists, are sorry to see. Countries are defined as virtuous or spendthrift, taking a Manichaean, stigmatizing stance, for which a priggish onlooker might be excused but not the governing classes called upon to support and enhance with due responsibility and long-sightedness the European political project, without letting that project become a burden for the populations in whose name it is allegedly being carried out.

We really seem to be dreaming: things that could quite calmly be explained to the man in the street are ignored by Europe's governing classes who have every reason, even in electoral terms, to understand and make it clear to their voters in the streets, factories, offices and banks that symmetry and cooperation in the financial field are, quite simply, more solid bases upon which to construct the dynamics of international trade, where what must count, even more than productivity, is the capacity of each country to have something to offer the others.

In a well-constructed system of international trade, every country involved has an interest in buying something from others, instead of producing it directly. Such is the 'law of comparative advantages', enounced not by a general but by a liberal economist, David Ricardo. It can be explained in terms of the advantages of productive specialization, and thus in terms of productivity, but, ultimately, it will suffice to consider the conditions of international trade to understand it. International trade is in equilibrium only when all countries import as much as they export. Otherwise, situations of structural deficit and surplus are created which polarize the traders, separating them instead of holding them together. Sooner or later, the need arises to buy from debtors simply to be able to continue selling. Symmetry is primarily an economic need, rather than a political or a moral one. On the other hand, persistent dissymmetry undermines economic conditions and aggravates political relations.

By the look of things, we have all the elements to prefer the intelligent solution to the present condition. And, on the basis of the clearing principle, we can also see more clearly the harm done by the pseudo-principle of liquidity. Failure to take on symmetrical obligations generates pressure to break relations between debtors and creditors, which in turn leads to the frantic search for insurance against the risk thus incurred. In short, when credit is granted with a procedure such that no one comes face-to-face with anyone else, there can be no trusting anyone. The saleability of risk has become a surrogate for the word given, the promise made and kept. Deals have been sealed in silence, even under the counter, indiscriminately with all, on the understanding that no one would ever be called upon to answer for their promises – until the situation exploded. It exploded in America with the sub-prime debtors who, despite their designation (sub-prime is the same as insolvent), were considered financeable only because their debts were saleable. And it exploded in Europe, where a country that should have been seen as financeable only within certain limits from the very outset was financed generously, and at giveaway prices, by the very same people who now wonder at its recklessness in running ever deeper into debt.

'I seem to be dreaming,' said the Lehman banker in the movie. The trouble with dreams is that sooner or later you wake up. This was quite clear to John Law, who devised one of the first systems based on the leverage and re-financing of insolvent debtors: my system works only if no one opens their eyes. Ultimately, however, people love truth and the light of day, and sooner or later Law has to sneak away in the dark.

The findings emerging from comparative analysis of the two principles upon which finance can be based may well prompt the thought that living through an epochal crisis somewhere after the point of no return is not, after all, such a bad thing. We were already badly off when we thought we were well off. The financial markets constituted a problem even when they were working due to the very way they were working, the way they supplied credit.

Today, we must choose whether to live in a house that is burning or in a house that still largely needs building. We can only hope that few of us feel the cold so badly that we would choose the burning house to keep us warm.

In choosing what to do in these conditions, there is no need to nurture hope, but only to take a hard look at what is going on, without illusions but with no vain cynicism. There is no deus ex machina to hope for; it's just a matter of approaching principles with open eyes.

New Signs

One might be tempted to say that this crisis, like any self-respecting crisis, hasn't spared the managing classes. There is some evidence: heads have fallen, and careers have been curtailed. But we need to be more precise. In democratic systems, no political group has the monopoly of authority and responsibility, and endeavouring to prove the contrary is basically puerile. Granted this is so, what we see is that the crisis has hit that part of the governing class that was in government when it broke out. Few governments have held out since then, regardless of their political colouring.

Far less shaken, on the other hand, are the ideological attitudes which have found ample endorsement over and above contrasts in alignment. The risk remains that in reality even that part of the governing class now standing as alternative to the governments enfeebled by crisis lacks truly alternative ideas. Well-intentioned as they may be, the risk is that their ideas prove insufficient, and insufficiently new, to foster changes going in the right direction.

As for the ideological framework of neoliberalism as it has developed over the last thirty years, cutting across political alignments, it has clearly taken a blow, at least according to the soft version of a faith in the efficiency of market logic as widespread as is the tendency to swallow it whole. By now, it's become a commonplace to say that the markets aren't always right. And yet a clear alternative has yet to emerge. So it's conceded that the markets aren't always fair, but they're strong, and they lord it over the state. Albeit grumblingly, we bow to their dictates.

Still strong, moreover, is technocratic temptation. Some see it as perfectly right to conceive the action of reform policy in terms of institutional tactics, to submit to the judgement of the markets in order to, as they say, attract investments. When it comes to reform, the volatility of market decisions is not ascribed in psycho-pathological terms to the quirks of agents that find justification in the markets, but, rather, prompts warnings to be extremely cautious in proposing any solutions that might risk displeasing investors, who seem to be just waiting to be allured by the 'right' decisions.

If we look at Italy, for instance, many reforms of the administrative machinery that tends to smother the real economy have long been wanting. What leaves us bemused, however, is the general acceptance that the markets should dictate the reform agendas. As long as they do, however, what should not surprise us is that their dictates have led to the disappearance from the agenda of the reform of finance, which was so widely advocated when the crisis set in.

In the meantime, of course, some new shibboleths have come in. Probably, and despite everything, it still makes a difference whether it's the left or the right that draws up the policy agendas. The right may be perfectly entitled to make do with the neoliberal ideological status quo. Perhaps. The left is clearly showing increasing unease with the 'reformist' approach that it's better if we (of the left) manage capitalism. The question to be addressed, however, runs: is it really a matter of 'saving capitalism from the capitalists'? Why on earth should it be? Perhaps because there are no alternatives to capitalism? But who says, or rather who has demonstrated, that a market economy must also be a capitalistic economy? Perhaps it really is, more modestly, a matter of saving the market from capitalism.

Assuming market economy and capitalism to be two quite distinct things, clearly if the neoliberal approach to the market were abandoned, the state approach would not in itself prove any more sound or attractive. Statism is certainly no better than marketism. We discussed at length the strange entanglement of state and market, specifically the case of the financial markets, in our previous book, *The End of Finance*.

Here we wish to make an even simpler point: marketism and statism are no longer roads that can seriously be taken. No one can really imagine now that growth can be achieved, today, with the deficit spending that characterized the earlier stages of growth. Not in the present situation, with states coming under the fire of markets precisely because, in order to save the markets, they have reached levels of debt that can no longer be increased as long as finance takes the form of globalized financial markets.

It is not a matter of enhancing the state's bargaining power vis-à-vis the financial market, inventing new instruments to borrow in the old way. Eurobonds are, after all, state bonds, and, given the liquidity logic, bonds both need the financial markets and make them possible. Perhaps we can't make do without them today, in which case it needs to be seen that European public debt bonds imply a federal European state exercising a European fiscal policy.

But perhaps we should really be rethinking the role of states in the light of the political significance of the reforms that can be made today. To bring in a real reform of finance, the states need not depend on the financial markets in any way. Indeed, the more fully the reform of finance transforms capitalistic market finance into finance for the market economy, the less will the public role of public bodies prove a merely supplementary economic one (deficit spending to boost demand) to become what it should ideally be – that of mapping the path ahead.

New watchwords, then, have in fact emerged, suggesting the will to open up new prospects. It remains to be seen, however, whether the will for regeneration rests on old principles, or whether the new watchwords will open the way for a project that can bring the economy to rest on more solid financial principles.

A programme of this sort can be summed up with three watchwords: re-localization, reorganization, cooperation. If re-industrialization is to be financially possible, and not reduced to a more or less covert policy of autarky, it must be possible for finance to relate to local production. If the idea is to re-localize production, while finance has become increasingly global, then the aim must also be a re-localization of finance. However, re-localizing finance implies redefining relations between finance and economy. It is, in fact, thanks also to the globalization of finance that the de-localization of production has come to hold sway as an economically efficient option. The criteria for the financing of firms, associated with the short-term financial rationale of cost-cutting, have favoured those firms that implement de-localization rather than those that have sought to safeguard that wealth of skills that is the heritage of every territory. By contrast, re-localized finance is necessarily a medium-to-long period finance favouring the maintenance of competitiveness through support for skills. And in principle, safeguarding the local patrimony of skills accords well with the Ricardian principle of comparative advantages: thus it does not compete with international trade, but actually implies a channel for it.

Seeing that inter-European trade accounts for a very considerable part of world trade, a policy in support of re-localization of production within the EU could lead to a strengthening rather than a thinning out of trade links between member states. And if we could conceive of a European economy based on strong local economies with close and intensive trade relations, the financial dimension could count for less. The crucial point is the 'adhesive' for the relations between states. Trade or finance? Cooperation between producers or covert distrust of debtors by creditors? The question is up for discussion.

Moreover, the very same questions arise if we turn our attention to the effects of the crisis on financial operators. Here, we come to an aspect that merits particularly close attention: the capacity for resistance to crisis, i.e., the 'resilience' of certain financial operators pronounced obsolete by neoliberal financial doctrine. Our reference here is to the world of cooperative credit. Due also to the handsome returns reaped by commercial banks, the cooperative forms of finance had been losing market and appeal until crisis broke out. They were seen as relics of a chummy rural past, doomed to be swept away by the cosmopolitan wind of innovation. And yet, in the wake of the crisis, it is precisely the world of cooperative credit that has best stood up to a credit crunch which, despite all the official reassurances from the banking world ('Tout va très bien, Madame la Marquise, there's no lack of credit for the deserving'), is crippling the small and medium-sized firms. The reason is easily found: their mission having been from the outset to serve a local area and mediate between savers and entrepreneurs who are already acquainted, and not to sell financial products that merit looking no one in the eye, these banks have never strayed from the local context, anticipating with their resilience the directions that reforms should take: supporting competence with a view to competition, and co-operation between debtors and creditors.

Furthermore, forms of cooperative finance self-managed by firms are proliferating. The name they are known by is corporate barter, or peer-to-peer lending. A study commissioned by the City of London has listed about seven hundred, while a French inter-ministerial committee has commissioned a study on the subject. In Italy, a small concern showing vigorous growth, Sardex, is promoting the same business, enjoying increasingly lively attention. Experiments in local currency are in the pipeline in France, England and Italy, often with the support of local administrations.

The signs are there, at all levels. What, then, is to be done to harmonize initiatives coming from all directions? Is it simply a matter of taking action, or hadn't we better do some thinking to make a good job of it?

Rethinking Economic Doctrine

Today, the need to rethink economic doctrine is becoming urgent. After all, a lack of hard economic thinking must be to blame if it proved possible to pass off the capitalistic financialization of the economy, and consequent accumulation of deficit, as a triumph of free market economy.

If the only tool you have is a hammer, everything tends to look like a nail, according to an old Japanese adage. If the model for economic activity lies in the profitability of securities, and if its objective is to guarantee payment of returns to rentiers, then the sole economic objective that can be pursued is growth. Are we sure that the economy exists to make finance possible? Might not the contrary be true?

This unresolved misunderstanding inevitably generates further misunderstandings. Today, when we play the 'growth' card against 'the rigour' imposed by the financial markets, do we really know what we're talking about? We should at least be able to say: there's growth and there's growth. There is growth made tremendously obligatory by the imperative to pay financial rent, and there's growth which is a blessing,

coming through labour and generated by it. The risk with
the growth now being invoked by all and sundry is that it
may take on purely financial form, developing at the expense
of labour and enterprise.

We have already seen this happening. Growth and
de-industrialization are not incompatible, at least not every-
where. The worldwide liquidity economy has functioned
thus. The American locomotive, which jammed in 2007, was
a locomotive that financed the production of others (the
Chinese one, if it needs spelling out). In an odd and misguided interpretation of the theory of comparative advantages, one country – the United States – specialized in the
production of debt, but in an international currency, namely
the dollar. This enabled others, the Chinese, to 'buy dollars'
in exchange for its commodities. Thus came about a strange
situation in which the emerging world producer also became
the net world creditor on condition, however, that payment
of debts never be demanded.

Europe has seen a variant of this bizarre condition that is
even more perverse in some respects. Carried out in a context
of European trade in balance with the rest of the world,
construction of the euro enabled the financial markets to
make no distinction any longer between the public debts of
the countries involved, denominated in euros, thereby making
it possible for the trade imbalances between eurozone countries to go on growing. The financial operators in the export-
ing countries financed the importing countries, and in so
doing rendered structural the very trade imbalances which
would have generated strong pressure on the pre-euro
exchange rates and so led to readjustment of the rates. Here,
too, a bizarre specialization came about at the expense of
any sound conception of international equilibrium.

Let us be clear: the only international economic situation
that merits the name of equilibrium is that in which the balances of trade of all those engaged in it eventually balance
out. No sound economic theory of international trade
can dispense with this condition, which is a matter not so
much of doctrine as, in the first place, of common sense.

Commodities are paid for with commodities, imports with exports. This is not a 'return to barter', but rather the foundation of market economy.

Unless, of course, money and credit are seen as commodities like any others. What happens in this case is that everyone 'specializes' in the production of something that is not a commodity – the relationship between debtors and creditors. The European crisis is a crisis in a relationship that got off on the wrong foot and which, precisely because it was not seen to be misconceived at the outset, now has creditors suddenly feeling justified in reproaching those they owe their status to, i.e. the debtors, without feeling duty-bound to recognize that the debtors were, to begin with, purchasers.

What 'growth' is it that concludes with divorce between partners who actually cannot divorce because they have become what they are only through relations built on the above assumptions? And above all, what growth should we be thinking of if we are to find our way out not only from this crisis but also, and above all, from the flawed relationships that had long been leading to it, even when things seemed to be going well for everyone, debtors and creditors 'happy ever after'?

Let us return to the science, or better, doctrine or, even better, economic doxa prevalent in these years. If we find ourselves in these straits, it is also because the euro was botched in the making, and it was made thus also with the blessing of economic theory. Economists contributed to making a bad job of the euro, giving their blessing to the financialization of relations between member states. Not, of course, all of them. But the critical voices that were in fact raised, even from the outset, got scant attention. The most worrying thing about the euro is the fact that it was born not from serious, rigorous debate, but with fanfares worthy of bygone military parades.

There's no point in naming names, nor, for that matter, in contemplating the void of a debate never held. What we must do now – now that the subject is to be broached – is to question why no need for it had been felt before.

The answer is simple and all too banal. If there's one subject that economic science in general has not approached in a way that might truly be termed scientific, it's money. The whole sorry state of affairs contemplated here was able to come about because the dominant economic doxa dogmatically assumed that money was a commodity like other commodities. It was on this point that debate was lacking, and on this point that it must open now if we are to find an alternative to a situation with no exit.

The need is to be able to combine rigour and growth in the name of, and thanks to, an appropriate conception of equilibrium. Now, in equilibrium money doesn't count. This is no newfangled idea, for it has always been there in sound economic doctrine. How can money fail to matter if it's treated as a commodity and a form of wealth, if financial relations are developed in terms of buying and selling money? With money freed from identification as a commodity, the role of the financial intermediaries is actually more determinate, both practically and scientifically, for they must contribute not to perpetuating but to re-absorbing imbalances between debtors and creditors.

Here we return to a point mentioned above. In this perspective, the work of readjustment is symmetrical and co-operative, precisely because the advantages of equilibrium apply to both sides. And, in this perspective, the purchaser not only gains an advantage but also does a favour to the seller, who otherwise would not have sold, and so produced, and so worked. In politics, perhaps, not all is relative, but in economics everything is clearly done in relation to others. The others are called counterparts, not because they are against us but because they are structurally different, and precisely for this reason essential to our economic existence. Economic competition does not exclude but entails financial cooperation. The pressure resulting from the fact that production and trade are conducted over time while uncertainty reigns implies the need to take on the task of adjustment jointly, and not try to shuffle off to others responsibilities that rest on either side.

Otherwise, we accept 'speculation' unprotestingly as a necessary evil. If Reagan could define the Soviet Union as 'the empire of evil' due to its economic system, are we now to put up with an ill-constructed finance that exerts undue pressure on the economy, sanctioning the existence of an 'empire of the lesser evil'?

In the film *Margin Call*, one of the many unscrupulous financiers justifies his role thus: 'they hate us, but without us they could never have lived beyond their means.' Again – but this time it isn't a film – a Goldman Sachs trader had this to say in January 2007:

> The entire building runs the risk of collapsing, but I don't feel so guilty after all: the true goal of my job is to make capital markets more efficient and to provide at the end of the process American consumers with the most efficient means to borrow money and finance their expenditure; it is therefore a job imbued with nobility, and modesty, and ethics. [...] It's incredible how good I am at convincing myself, isn't it?[6]

The myth of financial market efficiency is in the first place a scientific chimera, an ugly beast, born from the failure to control the relation between things and words. A market economy theory able to demonstrate with a fair degree of reasonableness that an extensive and well-structured competitive market produces the best prices for all, purchasers and sellers, is applied to things – money and credit – which can hardly be recognized as commodities. Once the dogmatic mess has been made, and money is declared to be a commodity like any other, everything follows through with perfect logic, and the financial markets can be hailed as temples of economic truth *tout court*. It is they that dispense merit and demerit to economic operators and states, simply by forming prices. But economic reality can only bear the misconstruction so far.

Then rejection comes, and its crisis and, ultimately, the liquidity trap.

The first trap to be escaped from is a conceptual trap. There are still some economists able to state the conditions for equilibrium in international trade, and they have started to speak up again, with some very convincing arguments, for example with regard to the unsustainability of the German positions on European trade imbalances and debt. As yet, few are inclined to heed them, simply because doing so now would mean admitting having been unwilling to do so before. This used to be considered a matter of 'human respect' – a 'respectable' name for the sense of shame.

Market Economy and Capitalism

Shame, however, does not suffice to account for the silence. There is also a conceptual blindness, terminological confusion being a major cause. We dedicated considerable attention to this in *The End of Finance*, but it is worth returning to it with even greater simplicity. The point is, until we have learnt to measure the difference between capitalism and market economy with due precision, it will indeed be hard to imagine alternatives that are both desirable and practicable.

Desirable and practicable alternatives mean, in the first place, alternatives that explicitly address the task of harmonizing the dimension of individual initiative and freedom with due attention to and care of the political dimension, which is a matter of the community in which every initiative and exercise of freedom can find scope. Harmonizing means precisely holding together different elements in the most consonant way, leaving them to their differences since it is precisely the difference that makes the profound economic and human interest of the combination.

Late twentieth-century and early twenty-first-century capitalism found sustenance in an old eighteenth-century fable that was tasteless at the time but now (a chance to give progress its due) seems thoroughly stale. Our reference here is to Mandeville's fable of the bees. The corresponding scientific myth is called 'heterogenesis of ends', to the effect that individual greed is the source of all common well-being. Period. And so it's... free for all!

Of course, Weber is right to brand as political infantilism the opposite assumption, namely that nothing but good can come of good intentions. Again, however, without taking a petit bourgeois viewpoint, there must be a possibility for some adventurous middle way. The middle way lies through a political adventure able to construct institutions such that pursuit of a common advantage does not oblige individuals to pursue objectives that cause them harm, and vice versa.

Returning to our leitmotif, this implies transition from capitalism to market economy. If capitalism is a market economy with one market too many, i.e. the financial market, the market economy becomes precisely what we would wish it to be, a place of competition on the basis of the efficiency of comparative advantages if, and only if, it is tempered by a cooperative finance.

We still have a long way to go in the direction of cooperative finance. Meanwhile, we must start from the present situation. Dispassionate analysis of the situation can yield precise evidence on both the urgency and the practicability and timing of transition to the cooperative principle. We have to understand just how capitalism threatens the market, and how the market can be saved from capitalism.

2

The Global Crisis and the Need to Reform the International Monetary and Financial System

The Crisis is Global

The crisis was born global and remains global. Today, Europe's problems have distracted attention from this fact, but the European drama is in reality only the second act of the tragedy that concerns the whole world. The global nature of the crisis lies not only in the causes that unleashed it and in the effects that followed, but also in the very nature of the financial system that made it possible.

Let us start with the causes. In recent years, we have become accustomed to speaking of a 'European sovereign debt crisis'. The expression seems to be justified by the fact that today the debts at risk of insolvency are those of certain European states. On closer inspection, however, even in relation to the sub-prime crisis that broke out in 2007, this is by no means a new crisis – it's the same ugly beast under a new guise. The Hydra has many heads, and no sooner is one cut off than two sprout in its place – or even more sometimes, as in this case. If we look back over the history of the last few years, even summarily, we can see all too well how today's public debts derived from yesterday's private debts. As we know, it all began in the United States, where, subsequent to the middle-class wage squeeze, with real wages

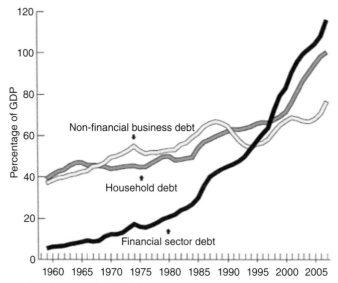

Figure 2.1 Private debts/GDP (percentages)
Source: Flow of Funds Accounts of the United States, Table L1 Market Debt Outstanding, Federal Reserve, and Table B-1, GDP, 1959–2007, Economic Report of the President, 2008, from: http://monthlyreview. org/2008/12/01/financial-implosion-and-stagnation

shrinking following Reagan's liberalizations, resort to credit began to grow. In twenty years, from 1985 to 2005, family debt doubled, from less than 50 per cent to nearly 100 per cent of gross domestic product (GDP) (Figure 2.1). 'Let us all be happy and live within our means, even if we have to borrow the money to do it with.' Artemius Ward's ironical aphorism found widespread practice, thanks to financial deregulation and the development of securitization, which allowed access to credit for even the most marginalized classes.[1]

Sub-prime debtors are, by definition, people unable to pay their debts; nevertheless, they were able to take out mortgages simply because the prices of the houses standing as guarantee went on rising, the value of the houses constantly appreciating in turn thanks to the steady increase in the number of people who, with the benefit of the mortgages, boosted demand...It was an ultra-modern revival of the

American dream, made accessible to all regardless of merit – massified, and hence betrayed.

It was a rude reawakening. The securitized sub-prime mortgages brought huge losses on the heads of the financial giants who had issued, bought or implicitly guaranteed them. The losses were literally incalculable since, there being no purchasers, the securities no longer had any price. The resulting uncertainty generated diffidence even among the financial intermediaries themselves. Contagion ran on from sub-prime to prime borrowers, and eventually credit was no longer forthcoming, even for debtors who had previously been judged perfectly solvent, and who had been able to borrow at the lowest rates. The banks ceased credit operations amongst themselves, and the inter-bank market froze. Having tried the 'hard line', letting Lehman go bust, the American government was obliged to intervene to save the other intermediaries. The British and Irish governments did likewise. With rescues and nationalization, private debts became public.

Nevertheless, the burden that the crisis threw upon the public finances was not limited to the cost of bail-outs. As the real effects of the financial crisis emerged, the bill grew longer. The credit crunch stifled consumption and investments. Incomes declined through bankruptcies and firing. Ill-concealed protectionism led to contraction of international trade. Consequently, increase in public spending was called for on all sides to support demand and mitigate the social effects of the recession, while tax revenues dipped together with incomes. Deficits widened and public debts grew in all the advanced economies (Figure 2.2).

Thus, the effects of the crisis also spread on a global scale. Some have tried to argue that only the western economies succumbed to crisis, and that those of the emerging countries, such as China, were left unscathed. Their arguments are unfounded, as is borne out by data on the BRICS slow-down. It could hardly be otherwise: these are export-led economies that inevitably suffer from stagnation in global demand. Moreover, this proves that even the most

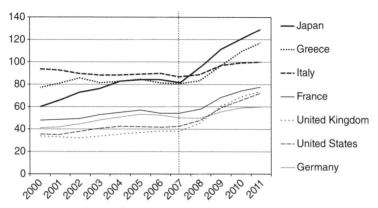

Figure 2.2 Public debts/GDP (percentages)
Source: Authors' calculations based on the International Monetary Fund, World Economic Outlook, October 2010

competitive countries, often hailed as examples of dynamism, are as vulnerable as the others, if not even more so, to international trends, as they depend on foreign demand for a significant share of their GDP. No country, great and strong as it may be, is independent of or indifferent to the vicissitudes of the rest of the world. In the ecumene of globalization, if a limb is sick, the whole body suffers.

But the real issue is far vaster. The trouble is, the crisis affects not only a limb but the lymphatic system that runs through the whole organism, serving to drain off excess liquids and prevent the formation of metastases. The international financial system is not simply the channel along which contagion is transmitted, but is itself the pathogen. In fact, those masses of debts now so hard to re-absorb could never have formed in the first place had it not been for the possibility to sell them off so easily on the global markets.

The problem, then, does not concern one side or another, but what keeps everything together. Today, the world is held together by the financial markets. Episodes of globalization have also occurred in the past. Traditionally, two others are recorded in the West: the first in the period of the so-called geographical discoveries, the second between the late nineteenth and early twentieth centuries. Common to all of them, including the present one, is a political and military dimension in which power relations are played out. However, at the strictly economic level, each shows its own peculiar characteristics. In this respect, in fact, the first globalization was characterized by the integration of trade; it was above all commodities that traversed the planet from side to side. The second also saw massive movements of capital, but mostly in the form of direct investments: money was on the move, but to find stable use in real, long-term investments for the development of industries and infrastructures in the then emerging countries. Only the present globalization has led to the emergence of portfolio investments with short-term capital movements: today, the vast majority of the money moving from one country to another does not serve to acquire goods or services, nor even to build factories or bridges, but to buy shares, bonds, currencies, derivative instruments or other financial assets that can be sold immediately afterwards. Capital is set moving on a scale hitherto unimaginable, and no longer with any relation to the movements of trade.

Thus, the 'third globalization' goes entirely under the colours of liquidity. The world is held together by financial markets, where international investments take liquid form, shifted and transformed at will. A singular and potentially toxic bonding agent, liquidity flows over the globe in a ceaseless quest for promising investment opportunities, expanding sectors, emerging countries, favourable fiscal regimes and accommodating economic policies. Arriving and departing, liquidity metes out rewards and punishments, granting its favours to firms and countries in growth, abandoning those it deems unreliable. Liquidity governs the fortunes of the world, its 'last judgement' running in a continuous cycle.

It is only over the last forty years that liquidity has established its regime with the progressive liberalization of international financial markets. Despite increasingly frequent and devastating crises, liberalization was able to proceed, thanks to an unfaltering faith in the efficiency of the financial markets – and massive interventions by the central banks.

Actually, without these interventions, the markets would have collapsed, and with them faith in their efficiency, a faith constantly in need of being shored up. Far from being that self-regulated market that neoliberal doctrine and economic theory love to picture, the financial market has proved to be in constant need of support from outside.[2] Without lavish replenishment by the central banks whenever they threatened to dry up, the markets would long ago have lost their liquidity. It is indeed significant that their extension, growth and liberalization on a global scale were accomplished only subsequent to the suspension of dollar/gold convertibility in 1971. It is only since then, in fact, that the central banks have been able to create money from nothing with no restrictions and so act as a 'source of liquidity to support the economic and financial system',[3] as Alan Greenspan programmatically put it at the beginning of his twenty-year stint as governor of the Fed, during which he pursued his mission taking pains worthy of a better cause.

By now, the point Keynes made back in 1936 should be clear to all: liquidity is a fetish – not only because it is artificial, not only because it is illusory, not existing for the community as a whole, and not only because it is there to be seen only as long as you believe in it, but also, and above all, because it compromises the investment system even when everything seems to be working. Liquidity hamstrings evaluation of investments in terms of their effective long-term profitability; it dissolves solidarity between creditor and debtor, and offers the creditor the illusory power to guard against every uncertainty the future may hold. Finally, it generates moral hazard. Economic theory recognizes moral hazard but fails to draw the one essential conclusion, namely that the monetary and financial system must be reformed to purge investments and money itself of the element of liquidity. Until this reform is put through, any other system of regulation will prove pure wishful thinking. For, as we will demonstrate, many of the problems that have given just cause for complaint over the last few years depend on liquidity: the inability of the banks to perform their function, the hypertrophic spawning of financial instruments totally divorced from the real economy, the astronomical bonuses going to the bankers, the inability of the rating agencies to assess the creditworthiness of debtors with due wariness, and the inexorable increase in global imbalances. We will review all these issues, demonstrating how they ultimately depend on the liquidity of financial markets, and how futile the dream is of settling them without having first constructed the entire monetary and financial systems on a different principle.

Lest we in turn, however, be suspected of wishful thinking, let us begin with some serious thinking about how a different system could work. This doesn't mean going far out of our way, for it will suffice to turn our thoughts once again to the actual functions served by capital movements and to how they were appropriately delimited only seventy years ago with the Bretton Woods Agreements.

What Do Capital Movements Move?

In keeping with his theoretical position, Keynes's plan for the post-war economic order included controls over capital movements. On this point, moreover, the Americans were in agreement, and at Bretton Woods it was effectively decided to control them. Indeed, at the closing ceremony of the Bretton Woods conference on 22 July 1944, the Secretary of the Treasury Morgenthau was able to affirm that the intention of the American administration was precisely to 'drive the usurious moneylenders from the temple of international finance'. The intention proved short-lived. By the end of the 1950s, international capital movements were already flourishing freely on the unregulated Eurodollar market. Indeed, by 1987, Guido Carli was able to point his finger at the 'rude irruption into the temple of international finance by those who had gone under the designation of usurers'.[4] People still had long memories in those days.

Today, at a distance of twenty-five years during which the liquidity of international capital has continued to increase exponentially in volume and extension, it would at least be worthwhile to reconsider the basic assumptions upon which the world economic order of the post-war period was to be constructed, without taking it for granted that the freedom of capital movements that has characterized the last forty years should be the norm.

Control does not mean prohibition. It is not a matter of banning every form of money transfer from one country to another. Rather, it is a matter of distinguishing between various types of transfers, authorizing some and prohibiting others. Basically, the transference of money from one country to another, or from one person to another, can serve three purposes: as donation, payment or loan. On donations in the form of international aid, which are in any case rarely of great proportions, there can be no discussion; acts of liberality should obviously be free. Nor, evidently, can there be much to discuss in the case of money transferred to pay for imports, thus corresponding to an equivalent transference of commodities in the opposite direction: either you bring in some trade policy to limit the purchase of goods or you allow for their payment. Basically, then, the question arises in the case of loans, i.e. transfers of money on capital account. These are what are called capital movements in the strict sense of the words. They are normally described as pure movements of money, with no counterpart in terms of commodities. However, it is a case that bears closer examination. Effectively, in this case no goods or services are obtained in exchange for money taken out of the country, but only a credit vis-à-vis the foreign debtor and the returns that credit yields in terms of dividends or interest. For the creditors, then, capital movements provide higher yield on their investments than they could earn at home. This, indeed, is the argument that is used to justify capital movements: the optimal allocation of capital at the global level with a view to maximizing returns. Capital, they say, must be able to flow freely towards higher returns. Such is the – perfectly understandable – point of view of the lender.

However, finance is a relationship between debtor and creditor, so let us also see how the debtor feels about the transference. In his case, apparently, the movements of capital respond to the corresponding need to obtain financing abroad that is not available at home. Actually, however, from the point of view of a country's economy as a whole, the demand for capital from abroad should correspond to a demand for commodities from abroad. There would be no need for foreign money to buy home produce. A country can always supply from within all the credit needed to finance the purchases of residents buying commodities produced by other residents, even if only in the form of deferred payment conceded by the latter. If there is a need for foreign currency, it should be to buy commodities from abroad. Consequently, when a country borrows abroad it should, after all, be to finance the purchase of commodities. Essentially, international credit should always be deferment of payment. The picture would be clearer if we saw capital movements not as transferences of money with no counterpart in commodities, but as transferences of commodities without immediate payment in cash. In any case, it is clear that, strictly from the point of view of accounting, movements of capital (net of their remuneration) must always be equal in amount and opposite in direction to movements of commodities. In fact, this is reflected in the balance of payments, which keeps track of movements of money in and out of a country, and where the current account is always equal and opposite to the financial account.

A country that buys more than it sells abroad depletes its currency reserves and increases its foreign debts for a total sum corresponding to its balance of trade deficit, while a country selling more than it buys abroad accumulates foreign reserves and credits in proportion to its trade surplus. Viewed from this perspective, movements of capital clearly can and must only be temporary. A country can contemplate 'living beyond its means', buying more than it is able to sell on international markets, only by drawing upon its reserves or borrowing abroad. Such behaviour is sensible and sustainable only if, sooner or later, the balance reverses and the country is able to pay its debts and replenish its reserves by selling more than it buys. The same applies, reversing the terms, to a creditor country. It can make sense for a country to sell to others more commodities than it receives in exchange only with a view to buying more than it sells sooner or later, and so spend the credits and currency reserves previously accumulated.

At Bretton Woods, capital controls met with favour on all sides but today, after forty years of international financial market liberalization, they have become taboo, almost as if controlling capital movements amounted to blind opposition to the economic function of capital. Now, we may grant that it's better not to ascribe to states the power to decide which foreign investments are to be allowed and which prohibited. But if we choose to leave it to the markets, they must be working properly. They needn't be 'good' in the absolute sense, on the basis of some undefined and possibly undefinable moral criterion; it will suffice if they are 'good at' performing the function that economic theory sees them ideally as serving – getting funds to firms. However, this would entail that every movement of capital, including at the international level, should in due course be followed by a movement in the opposite direction. In other words, every movement of capital should take the form of an advance with a view to payment.

It is indeed significant that movements of capital are nil, in equilibrium, in all theories of international economy. This is the necessary condition for exchange rates to settle at purchasing power parity or, to put it simply, for the workers in every country to be able to earn their bread without having to emigrate. But it is also the right condition for production and trade to develop, at the international level, in accordance with the principle of comparative advantage, or in other words leaving each to concentrate on what they are able to do best, thereby contributing to the well-being of all in the best possible way. On the other hand, if there are capital movements which generate persistent imbalances, then the international division of labour leads to different outcomes and some countries will specialize in the production of debts...

Capital Markets Ought to be Less Liquid

Capital markets need to be made less liquid, not more.[5] Keynes had long ago called for the introduction of a tax on financial transactions in *The General Theory*. Today, it is sometimes referred to as the 'Tobin tax'. Actually, this is not the right term for it. The tax proposed by James Tobin at the beginning of the 1970s was to have been applied to the conversion of one currency to another, the idea being to reduce variations in exchange rates which had been left free to fluctuate after Richard Nixon took the dollar off the gold standard in 1971. The tax being mooted today should apply to all financial operations, not only on the currency market. In practice, then, it should apply to the purchase and sale of all kinds of financial asset: shares, bonds and derivatives. But this is precisely what Keynes was contemplating in chapter 12 of *The General Theory*: 'The introduction of a substantial Government transfer tax on all transactions might prove the most serviceable reform available with a view to mitigating the predominance of speculation over enterprise.'[6]

It would, therefore, be more appropriate to call it the 'Keynes tax'. Be that as it may, it is not so much the name as the sense of such a tax that concerns us here. Many of its advocates insist on the fact that it would be a way to 'make finance pay at least part of the costs of the crisis it has caused'. However, its real merit does not lie here. Indeed, as long as it is proposed as a way to punish bankers, it will come up against their opposition as well as the opposition of all the interest groups they represent. And as long as governments depend on the banks and financial markets for their financing, they are hardly likely to put restrictive measures on them. It is precisely this insistence on the punitive, not to say vengeful, nature of the 'Tobin tax' that constitutes the major obstacle to its adoption. Thus, what is vaunted as the greatest merit of a tax of this kind actually constitutes its worst flaw.

On the other hand, what opponents of the tax decry as the most serious limitation of the 'Tobin tax' is in reality its greatest virtue. The main objection to a financial transaction tax is the assertion that it would trigger a flight of capital from the country that is intending to introduce it unilaterally. If a country taxes financial transactions, they say, those transactions will be transferred to another market. But this is precisely the point: it would be the transactions that would be shoved off, not the capital. In fact, since it applies to the transference and not to the possession of a financial asset, the tax would not hit people buying securities in order to keep them so much as purchasers who mean to sell them. The rates contemplated are very low. For example, the proposal advanced by the European Commission in September 2011 suggests a tax of 0.1 per cent on the purchase/sale of shares and bonds, and 0.01 per cent on the notional amount in derivative contracts.[7] Clearly, such a tax would be negligible for anyone wanting to buy a financial asset to keep for the returns it yields, but it could prove far from negligible for anyone buying it with the intention of selling it in turn in the short term in order to make a capital gain, thanks to a rise in market price. In other words, the closer the investors' time horizon, the steeper the tax would prove. For the so-called 'high-frequency traders', i.e. those who engage in arbitrage, buying a security to sell it a few hours – or even a fraction of a second – later, a tax of this sort would prove downright prohibitive. In short, a financial transaction tax would hit the speculators but not the investors, the expression 'speculators' for once no longer being, as is so often the case, simply an epithet evoking shady financiers plotting behind the scenes, but a technical term unambiguously denoting the business of short-term investors who buy and sell bonds with no professional concern for the prospects of long-term returns on the underlying real investment. If this is so, then the effect of the tax would not be to scare off all capital, but only the most volatile.

The 'Tobin Tax' in One Country

It is therefore illogical to reject the financial transaction tax on the grounds of the alleged loss of foreign investments it would entail. It would be like saying we won't introduce a tax on polluting emissions because it would drive the polluting firms away. Keeping the polluting firms away is, in fact, the primary aim of such a law, not an undesired side effect. If you don't want the law, it means you want pollution: if you don't want the tax on financial transactions, it means you want that form of economic pollution that speculation assuredly is.

This is why the so-called 'Tobin tax' can be introduced even in a single country without necessarily waiting for an international agreement. Moreover, if unanimity were really necessary to avoid the flight-of-capital risk, it is hard to see why it should suffice to adopt the tax at the European level. What would be the use of an agreement in the eurozone or even in the entire European Union if the rest of the world remained exempt? But if, on the other hand, it were seen as a useful means of fighting speculation, then the need would be for unhesitating adoption by any country that deemed it right to repress speculation. It could be argued by the same token that no country should adopt restrictions on child labour until all the others have, for otherwise it would risk de-localization of production to countries lacking any such restrictive legislation, where labour costs would be lower. This, however, is a line of reasoning that is not only immoral, subordinating justice to efficiency, but also anti-economical since, if it were adopted on the worldwide scale, it would eventually mean forgoing justice entirely with no gain in terms of efficiency.

Liquid Capital Markets Imply Flexible Labour Markets

The example presented above is not all that paradoxical. In principle, the liquidity regime requires perfect mobility for all its factors, not only capital. It is no mere chance that liberalization of capital markets has gone ahead hand-in-hand with flexibilization of labour markets. Labour must be made as liquid as money. It is indeed significant that the advocates of labour market reform include a central banker like Mario Draghi, who has no jurisdiction in the matter at the formal level. Where money and credit are commodities, labour needs to be so, too.

According to Karl Polanyi, labour and capital, like land, are fictitious commodities: factors of production that cannot be considered as commodities since they have not been produced and have been reduced to commodities only by dint of the movement – ideological and political at the same time – that has led to the construction of capitalism.[8] This movement, Polanyi deems, came under way during the globalization of the late nineteenth century and was slowed down by the emergence of socialist, cooperative and trade unionist 'counter-movements', proceeding to the rise of mixed economies and welfare states in the post-war period. As we can see today, it was the very same movement that geared up once again with the globalization of the late twentieth century, leading to liberalization of all markets, and in particular of the productive factors: capital, raw materials and labour.

The transformation into commodities of what are not in fact commodities is not accomplished without consequences: it deprives money of its characteristic as common measure for trade, making it the object of a potential accumulation that hampers trade and production; it deprives credit of its characteristic as a mutual relationship between creditor and debtor, transforming it into a negotiable security that relieves creditor and debtor of all responsibility with regard to its effective payment; it deprives nature of its quality as common, inappropriable asset, exposing it to reckless exploitation with no concern for its preservation, generating such violent fluctuations in the prices of raw materials as to jeopardize the subsistence of producers and consumers; and finally it deprives labour of the dignity that comes with competence, delivering it up to the precariousness generated through competition.

The globalization of liquidity entails the indiscriminate liberalization of every market, the forced flexibilization dictated by the so-called structural reforms, and the globalization of precariousness in employment, environment and finance. If the commercialization of labour is to be resisted, then the commercialization of money and credit must also be rejected. Money and finance need to be purged of liquidity if work is to be freed from precariousness and an even more radical counter-movement achieved from capitalism to the market economy.

The Banks are No Longer Doing Their Job

The attack waged by finance on work does not even spare the work of finance. Finance used not to consist entirely of financial markets, but comprised at least two basic elements: banks and stock markets. Today, the stock markets dominate the financial system, meeting with no resistance. True, the banks are still there, but they are increasingly being reduced to simple stockbrokers. Establishing long-term credit relations is an increasingly marginalized function in their trade, the purchase and sale of securities playing an increasingly central role. The traditional virtue of the banks, based on the exercise of prudence, is giving way to a new version, based on the management of liquidity.

The banks used to conceive of themselves as intermediaries between savers and investors, and put the conception into practice. On the one hand, they received savings, i.e. the money of people whose incomes exceeded their expenditure – essentially households – while on the other hand they set about finding a use for that money for those who needed more than they had at their disposal – essentially firms. The main function of the banks was to link up savings and investments, households and firms, transforming savings into investments and so boosting the circulation of money so that it would always be in the hands of those who had the best use for it.

This was the most evident function, although possibly not the most important. As Schumpeter taught us, the banks did not confine their activities to transferring money and boosting circulation but they also created money through the mechanism of fractional reserve banking. Being bound to retain only a minimal part of the deposits and cash, the banks could in fact advance to firms a greater quantity of money than they had effectively received. Thus, through the creation of bank money, the banks were able to finance not only the circulation of commodities already produced but also the invention and production of entirely new ones. Therefore the banks constituted the source of all possible innovation driving economic dynamics: the 'ephors of capitalism'.[9]

In theory, it is still like this but, if we look at what banks are effectively doing, we will have to use the past tense. In fact, the function performed by the banks today is often the diametric opposite: rather than creating money and easing its circulation, they contribute to its stagnation and, in practice, its destruction, removing it from circulation.

Today, the banks act as sponges for the liquidity created by the central bank. On 16 November 2011, twenty-five managing directors of the major European banks met Draghi over lunch and asked him for money. On 8 December, the ECB Governing Council decided upon an unlimited supply of 36-month loans at a rate of 1 per cent. For Christmas, 523 banks applied for and received 489 billion euro through the 'longer-term re-financing operation' as soon as it was made available.

Some held that the idea had already been put forward by Trichet.[10] Actually, this too can be traced back to a proposal by Keynes aimed at reducing long-term interest rates.[11] Clearly, however, Keynes's intention was that the money should ultimately serve to finance creditworthy firms. Significant in this respect is his exchange with the governor of the Bank of England, Montagu Norman, in May 1930. Responding somewhat defensively, the latter observed 'it would at present be hard to find many "approved enterprises"'.[12] Keynes came up with a memorable rejoinder: 'Surely they cannot maintain that England is a finished job, and that there is nothing in it worth doing on a 5 per cent basis.'[13] He added that it was up to the governor to single out deserving investments as president of the Bankers' Industrial Development Company, which had been instituted just a month before precisely with that task.[14]

The difference between the two approaches is crucial; it depends on whether it is borne in mind from the outset that loans are to be paid back or, on the other hand, it is forgotten. Keynes never lost sight of the need for repayment, and for this very reason tied the supply of loans to the financing of productive investments. The preference today is to forget it. To access ECB loans, banks simply have to deposit securities as guarantee. Determining which securities are eligible is left to the discretion of the national central banks. So how will the banks pay back the loans granted by the ECB within three years? Might not all this money generate inflation in the meantime? What are the chances that it will feed a speculative bubble on the financial markets? All these questions have remained unanswered or, rather, have been pushed aside.

So it was that the eurozone banks that had absorbed nearly 500 billion euros in ECB loans in December 2011 requested, and received yet more, at the end of March 2012 (Figure 2.3).

Where did all this money end up? Only a tiny fraction went into financing firms. A good part was invested by the banks in government bonds. Fine, you may say, just what the ECB expected: prevented by statute from buying government bonds directly, it lends money to the banks for them to do so. But it isn't all that fine. Relief for the cost of the public debt has proved minimal – in the case of Portugal, it actually increased to begin with: the yield on 10-year bonds rose over 17 per cent.

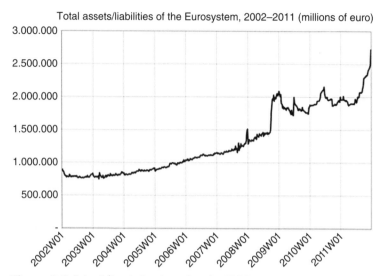

Figure 2.3 Liquidity injections by the ECB
Source: ECB, 'Consolidated Financial Statement of the Eurosystem', Statistical Data Warehouse (http:sdw.ecb.int)

In the meantime, the banks profited from the difference: it's a walkover for bankers when you can borrow 1,000 billion euros from the central bank at 1 per cent interest and invest it at 17 per cent in government bonds. Of course, these days (and at these rates!) there is always the risk of states going bankrupt, too, but who could blame the bankers if they were to? As Keynes famously said, 'worldly wisdom teaches that it is better for the reputation to fail conventionally than to succeed unconventionally'.[15]

In any case, as a matter of 'prudence', a good part of the money borrowed from the ECB was simply re-deposited. In the course of 2011, the eight major European banks increased their central bank deposits by 50 per cent, from US$543 billion to US$816 billion[16] (Figure 2.4).

Better, of course, a negative yield than the risk of incalculable losses. The pity is that precisely this attitude contributes to making such losses more probable. By failing to lend money to firms, the banks play their part in further

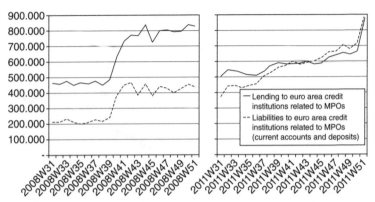

Figure 2.4 'Spitting in the wind': money lent by the ECB to European banks and re-deposited with the ECB, end 2008 and end 2011 (millions of euros)
Source: ECB, 'Consolidated Financial Statement of the Eurosystem', Statistical Data Warehouse (http:sdw.ecb.int)

depressing economic activity, jeopardizing the health of the still healthy firms and making payment of debts already granted more difficult.

The problem does not, as we have said, lie in the behaviour of banks. It's a structural problem, for it is the structure of the financial system, based on liquidity, which obliges the banks in the name of an ill-founded prudence to stop performing their real function. This, moreover, is exactly the meaning of the downgrading inflicted on a great many banks by Moody's on 16 February 2012, motivated by the fact that the banks have to reckon with, among other things, 'increased regulatory requirements' that have 'diminished these institutions' longer-term profitability and growth prospects'. The greater the demands made upon banks in terms of solidity and prudence, the higher is the risk of depriving firms of lifeblood, i.e. credit, weakening the economy and again in turn the banks themselves.

If the banking system as a whole is to follow a different rationale, the need is for a reform able to purge not only the financial market but also money itself of its liquidity, which, in the case of money, means its capacity as a store of value. One possible approach to the task might be, for instance, for the ECB to charge banks for the reserves they hold in excess of obligatory reserves. This would be a sort of negative interest rate to apply to the money that banks could lend but decide to keep. If there were a cost of this sort to holding money created by the ECB, the banks would have a concrete incentive to put it effectively into circulation.[17]

With the present system, however, there is also room for banks following different principles, above all in the countries of continental Europe where the financial system has traditionally been centred more closely on banks than on stock markets. Despite the liberalization introduced over the last few decades, banks continue to have a preponderant weight in the financial system of these countries. Moreover, while it is true that here, too, commercial banks and investment banks have seen progressive transformation into market operators, there remains a significant proportion of cooperative banks whose activities still consist above all in establishing long-term relations, even when supplying short-term credit (Table 2.1).

The cooperative banks have in general shown relatively better solidity and profitability in times of crisis, thanks

Table 2.1 Cooperative banking market share

	Deposits			Credits		
	2004	2009	2011	2004	2009	2011
In market-based systems						
– UK	2.0	2.0	2.2	1.3	1.4	1.6
– US	17.4	11.6	8.3	n.a.	n.a.	n.a.
In bank-based systems						
– France	50.2	41.5	46.2	53.7	46.5	56.0
– Germany	18.5	19.3	19.4	11.6	16.8	17.5
– Italy	29.2	33.3	33.9	25.9	30.8	31.7

Source: K. Mettenheim, 'Back to Basics in Banking Theory and Varieties of Finance Capitalism', *Accounting, Economics and Law* 3(3): 370

precisely to the fact that a smaller share of their assets is employed in the market and exposed to its volatility. It is also in consideration of this aspect that relationship banking, as it is known, is finding increasing favour in countries where it has traditionally operated on a smaller scale, such as the United Kingdom and the United States.[18]

Million Dollar Bonus

Since the crisis broke, few proposals for reform have met with such favour as the calls to change the criteria for evaluation and remuneration of bankers. Many concur that the bankers have been paid too much, that they have been too reckless and that all this has contributed to swelling a bubble destined to burst. In some cases this attitude has come close to the spirit of a witch-hunt. The paradox is that, despite all the fervour, not only have we witnessed dismal failure in reining in bankers' recklessness, but also an abject failure to change the rules on the basis of which their work is evaluated and paid.

Why has it so far proved impossible to introduce ceilings to banker bonuses? In part, we have to thank the opposition from the banks themselves who argue that any such measures would keep the best talents away. It is in fact clear that, at least so far, the bank lobbies have had the power to prevent the adoption of measures they hold counterproductive. In the light of the losses that some of these 'talents' have succeeded in inflicting on their own banks, even quite recently, one may reasonably doubt whether the present systems of incentives are really the right way to promote productivity and merit.

The competitive market is meritocratic, and so characterized by a particular form of justice. But meritocracy is not the only principle of justice: in fact, even within market economies, the need is recognized to temper the criterion of merit with that of need. Nevertheless, the market does clearly have the distinct merit of being able to recognize and reward merit: the better you are, the more money you make.

But that's not how financial market works. In fact, it's just the reverse: the more money you make, the better you are. The only measure of quality for the financial operator is the amount of money made.

On top of this, we have a further anomaly in the financial market. As pointed out by François Morin, the financial market is the only one that purchasers run to when prices rise,[19] and for a very simple reason: the 'commodities' traded on this market, i.e. securities, are not bought to satisfy a need, but to be resold. To put it in the terms of the classical economists, they have no value in use, but only value in exchange. This means that demand for such 'commodities' is limited neither by the satiety factor, which even sets a limit to the purchase of cherries when enough have been eaten, nor by the substitution factor, which switches purchase from cherries to strawberries when the former get too dear.

The more liquid they are, the closer financial assets come to cherries which are produced not to be eaten but to be continually bought and sold. Like the tins of salmon in a Yiddish anecdote that Moni Ovadia is wont to tell, securities are not made to be consumed – i.e. paid out – by the date of expiry, but to circulate on the market indefinitely.

The liquidity of securities makes the 'soundness' of the underlying investment irrelevant, so there is no need to be able to evaluate them in order to trade in them. The closer bankers come to being traders, the less they are expected to make any such evaluations. They only have to be good at selling – and on a very particular market where there are only merchants. Hardly anyone buys to keep now; everyone buys to sell in turn. Only one 'quality' of the product matters, namely its saleability. So everyone is happy on this market as long as prices keep rising, and the merits of each individual actor are assessed according to his or her ability to share in the gains.

Over and above merit, gains become the criterion for justice. Have they ever arrested a banker who was making money for the way he made it? As long as you make money, you're not only clever, but you have justice on your side. The real crime is to lose. The story of Bernard Madoff is paradigmatic in this respect, and deserves a brief digression.

The Unstrange Case of Bernie Madoff

Over the years of his honourable career, Madoff had made himself a reputation in an environment where reputation is everything. One of his firm's mottos went: 'the owner's name is on the door.' And the name of Madoff was considered a guarantee, to the extent that he merited the nickname 'Jewish T-bill' in New York's Jewish community.[20]

Madoff's strategy focused on the pursuit of returns that may not have been high but were sure, concentrating investment in securities representative of the most traditional stock exchange indexes. Madoff also dealt in derivatives, but with the sole aim of passing on any particularly high gains (and losses) in exchange for more limited but also more certain returns. Thanks to this strategy, a fund of his was for nearly twenty years able to offer average returns of 10% per year – lower than the 20–30% offered by more aggressive funds in boom years, but able to hold out even during downturns. And indeed in November 2008, the same fund was still declaring returns of 5.6% over the previous year, while the S & P 500 had fallen by 38%.[21]

Adopting wary, conservative investment strategies did not hold Madoff back from being at the cutting edge of technological innovation in the financial world. To enhance his competitiveness as a broker, he devised an electronic system for the diffusion of stock quotes, making a decisive contribution to the development of technology that was to constitute the telematic infrastructure of NASDAQ (the National Association of Securities Dealers Automated Quotations). As one of its five promoters, Madoff has also held office as chairman of the NASDAQ board of directors. In this role, as we read on his company's internet site, he was praised by one of the major US financial journals for having helped 'to make NASDAQ a faster, fairer, more efficient and more international system'.

Moreover, Madoff's integrity was widely recognized beyond financial circuits. Besides setting up the Madoff Family Foundation, he donated millions of dollars to various kinds of philanthropic organizations, in particular those representing the city of New York and the Jewish community. In short, a man above all suspicion.

Actually, for at least ten years, there had been some doubts about the lawfulness of Madoff's methods. In 1999, Harry Markopolos had written a letter to the SEC (the US Securities and Exchange Commission), stating that Madoff's company was 'the world's largest Ponzi scheme'. Of course, it may have been that Markopolos was simply a jealous and spiteful competitor. It remains to be seen why on earth the case opened by the SEC was subsequently closed in 2007 with no charges brought against Madoff.[22]

Shortly before bankruptcy, Madoff's company had assets estimated at US$13 billion. Only US$1 billion appeared to have been invested in stocks and shares. So what had become of the rest? The company claimed that it converted most of the assets into cash at the end of every quarter, but there is no evidence as to where all the cash might have been held.[23]

Madoff Securities was one of the major Wall Street brokers and an investment fund of considerable proportions. The auditors appointed to examine and certify the accounts were an unknown New York firm called Friehling & Horowitz, with an office of 24 square metres and a staff of three, including a secretary and an 80-year-old partner residing in Florida.[24] The only active partner regularly registered with AICPA, the US auditors association, had since 1993 made yearly declarations to the association that he had not carried out any auditing, and therefore was not subject to the monitoring that the association performs on its members.[25]

Various philanthropic organizations that had invested heavily in Madoff Securities suffered huge losses on its collapse. At the same time, these organizations may well have constituted the secret of its success, as long as it lasted. In fact, a US federal law obliges foundations to allocate at least 5 per cent of their assets every year to their statutory purposes. Given, however, that one purpose of foundations is to keep the founder's name alive and avoid digging into the assets, their administrators found the prospects of slender but sure gains offered by Madoff quite attractive enough. Conversely, it was thanks to the foundations' money that Madoff was able to count on reliable subscribers who wouldn't threaten to withdraw their investments at a moment's notice.[26] Ironically, therefore, as has been argued, these foundations constituted the actual foundation of an authentic 'philanthropic fraud'.[27]

For all these reasons, it was possible for the true nature of Madoff's activities to remain concealed for years until the fateful moment when many of the investors decided to withdraw their investments as the global liquidity crisis broke out. By the end of 2008, the company found itself having to cope with requests for a total of seven billion dollars. On 11 December, Bernard Madoff confessed to his sons, both directors in what had retained the nature of a family firm, that the company lacked the resources to meet the investors' requests for reimbursement, and that the whole thing was 'one big lie...a gigantic Ponzi scheme'.[28] His sons reported him to the US Securities and Exchange Commission (SEC). Bernard Madoff's secret shattered on the rocks of the crisis, and with it his financial and human fortunes. With the sobering spectacle of the vast abyss that opened under his feet, one can only wonder how Madoff's system could possibly have lasted so long.

Actually, Bernard L. Madoff Investment Securities LLC had been the object of investigation by the SEC and various other monitoring bodies at least eight times over the past sixteen years. In 1992, Madoff was involved in an investigation into the case of two Florida accountants accused of selling unregistered securities offering guaranteed returns between 13.5 per cent and 20 per cent. Part of the funds thus reaped was managed by Madoff, who stated, however, that he was unaware that the money had been raised illegally. 'With no investors found to be harmed, the SEC concluded there was no fraud.'[29] And in practice this must have been how the SEC judged matters in the subsequent cases, too...until harm eventually came to the investors.

So what eventually led to the discovery of the fraud? Bankruptcy. The day of judgement came only after the crisis, despite the fact that there was an authority designated for supervision and preventive intervention.

'The SEC said it is not clear when Madoff started using new investments to create the appearance of profits. But the alleged ruse was finally exposed by the global financial crisis.'[30] This means that the supervisory body had failed to detect any illegality in Madoff's activities until the crisis finally exposed it. The beginning of the fraud could only come to light at the end. After all, if the fraud proved invisible to the authority in charge of surveillance, who else should or could have seen it? Perhaps not even the man who invented it, the evidence seems to suggest. In fact, the statement by the SEC appears to imply that, as long as the financial market is expanding, there is no way to distinguish between a solid, honest enterprise and a thriving racket.

The problem was raised in fairly explicit terms by a columnist of the *Bloomberg News*, Jonathan Weil: 'After all, Madoff's scheme – at least in spirit, if not in its nefarious intent – wasn't much different than the business models at some of the nation's largest failed financial institutions.'[31] Without judging on mere intent, it's at the level of fact that the journalist was able to make a by no means far-fetched comparison, citing the case of the American International Group (AIG) which, before rescue by the government, had decided to distribute dividends at the very same time as it unveiled plans to raise US$12.5 billion in fresh capital. 'Whether you call that a Ponzi scheme or something less sinister, AIG was paying old investors with money raised from new investors.'[32]

Why, then, was it only Madoff who ended up behind bars (at least for now)? One good reason, of course, is that he confessed. But shouldn't it be the task of a supervisory body to expose fraud before the culprits confess or go bankrupt? A clue as to the reason why this, at least in some cases, does not happen may in fact be found in a speech given by the SEC Chairman, Christopher Cox: 'When the government becomes both referee and player, the game changes rather dramatically for every other participant. Rules that might be rigorously applied to private sector competitors will not necessarily be applied in the same way to the sovereign who makes the rules.'[33] The observation seems particularly apt coming at the end of a year, 2008, in which the federal state had used about US$6,500 billion of public funds to rescue firms and banks in crisis. And we can detect indeed a certain embarrassment in the words of the man at the head of a supervisory body of a government that should act as regulator but is increasingly an interested party.

But perhaps there is still not quite enough embarrassment and frankness in Cox's observations: the chairman of the SEC should also explain how on earth it was that, until the recent wave of interventions, when the US financial system was still entirely private and faithful to 'America's dedication to individual freedom', the swindlers were nevertheless able to get away with it indiscriminately. It may have been because, well before any direct participation in companies' capital, the sovereign state had a direct interest in the market continuing to grow in order to finance the twofold deficit in public finances and external accounts – even if it meant some indulgence towards those contributing to growth by selling securities illegally.

Perhaps Madoff's spokesman was being too modest when he went on to define him, after his arrest, as 'a longstanding leader in the financial services industry'.[34] Madoff truly incarnates the spirit of a financial system that is inextricably public and private, and precisely for this reason totally self-referential.

Sub-Prime 2: The Return

One might well have hoped that the inglorious end of the Bernie Madoff saga would prompt some thinking – and not only for him. And yet only a few years later, the merry-go-round is spinning once again. And the technique is the very same that led to the outbreak of crisis five years ago: securitization.

In the United States, it seems, they are trying to exit from the crisis – by the back door. The generous liquidity injections by the central bank have contributed to recreating that profusion of money that had characterized the pre-crisis scene. So do have we an ideal return to an ideal condition? Yes, the perfect setting for a new crisis.

Since the crisis broke out, the Fed has done its utmost to slacken credit conditions: it has increased the quantity of money threefold, eased up conditions for banks to obtain re-financing from it, reduced the standard interest rates to close to zero and stated its intention to hold them at that level 'for an extended period of time'. Enjoying access to cheap money over a fairly long time horizon, it shouldn't be difficult for the banks to find sufficiently safe and remunerative investment opportunities. Unfortunately for them, the US banks, unlike their European counterparts, cannot make do with the purchase of government bonds since the US debt offers very modest returns. It isn't that public accounts are straighter in the United States than in Europe, but simply that government debt securities are bought directly by the central bank without involving the other banks. So what, then, can banks do to make the best of the money that they in turn can receive at low cost from the Fed? Lend it? Yes, this would, of course, also be what they are meant for. But with so many uncertainties weighing on a still all-too-sluggish recovery, lending is a risky business – buying CMOs (collateralized mortgage obligations) is a much better option.

In the early months of 2011, the CMOs held by US banks increased by 20 per cent, from US$400 to US$480 billion.[35] The S & P forecast for 2012 was an increase of no more than 1 per cent in the loans supplied to firms.[36] Evidently, the US banks are far more interested in buying CMOs than in financing firms.

So what exactly are these CMOs? The initials stand for 'collateralized mortgage obligations', guaranteed mortgage credits: securities issued on the basis of a portfolio of other securities, in turn covered by mortgage loans. On the basis of the returns on the latter, CMOs are created with a diversified range of risk and returns to satisfy the purchasers' diverse requirements. And there are purchasers aplenty, attracted by returns well above the yield offered by government bonds. If you have read the sub-prime post-mortems, all this will ring a disturbingly familiar bell. Under a different acronym, a practice is spreading that echoes perfectly the practice developed with CDOs (collateralized debt obligations) and MBSs (mortgage-backed securities) in the days of the sub-prime mortgage bubble. Indeed, the description given by Steven Abrahams of Deutsche Bank leaves little room for doubt about the close family relationships shown by these types of instruments: 'The CMO business involves buying mortgage-backed securities, dividing them into pieces and then selling the sum total of the pieces at a higher price.'

Is that so? Let us remember that a car is worth less than the sum of its parts only when it's stopped running, as carbreakers know perfectly well. How long must we wait for this new form of securitization to fold as well?

Rating Agencies, and How to Live Without Them

With securitizations, the banks have ceased not only to lend but also to assess creditworthiness, and so this task, too, has been taken over by others, namely the rating agencies. The rating agencies have now taken the place of banks in evaluating the creditworthiness of debtors. What does it matter, you might think, provided someone does it? But it isn't all the same whoever does it. If assessment is made by a bank, the bank will bear the consequences because it enters into a long-term relationship with the debtor on the basis of that assessment. If the assessment proves erroneous and the debtor goes bankrupt, the bank loses out – in money, reputation and clients. On the other hand, if the rating agency gets its assessment wrong, it suffers no loss. Not in monetary terms, at any rate. If anything, it might lose face a bit, as has been the case during the crisis. But the face it is left with is evidently more than enough since the loss of reputation does not lead to a loss of clients, and thus of revenue, because, to begin with as we all know, the rating agencies do not exactly work in a context of perfect competition where mistakes lead to loss of clients who turn to competitors: actually, three big agencies share the entire market. Above all, however, it is because the clients of the agencies are not the creditors, who stand to lose out on over-generous assessments, but the debtors, who stand to gain. In other words, as has in fact been observed, the rating agencies operate in a threefold conflict of interest: the firm subjected to assessment is at the same time the party that pays for it, supplies the information necessary for its performance and, often, takes advice from the agency itself on how to improve its rating. Clearly, then, a rating agency has nothing like the incentive to perform the strict and thorough assessment that a bank has. And on top of this limited incentive, the rating agency is not nearly so well acquainted with the client. Indeed, given the type of work it has to do, the agency's acquaintance with the firm may be solely 'on paper', starting with the balance sheets and documents, while if the bank makes a good job of it, it can count on acquaintance with the firm based on close and lasting personal relations.

There is an exception worth noting to the rule that rating agencies are paid by the parties subjected to assessment: namely, that of the sovereign states. These latter are not too keen to be assessed; indeed, as we have recently seen, they may even ask not to be assessed.

It may seem hypocritical to ask not to be assessed precisely when assessment is negative, and indeed it is. If you want to contest the validity of a method of assessment, you should have the courage to do so when the assessment is positive. Nevertheless, the fact remains that, even in the case of sovereign states, the method is not equipped to produce a fair and just evaluation. Here, in fact, judgement proves equally distorted, albeit the other way around, and equally irresponsible. In this case, the agencies have nothing to lose in passing excessively harsh sentences. Indeed, by decreeing the down-grading of a country, they contribute, in practice, to making its debt unsustainable, thereby raising the cost of its financing on the market.

Given this state of affairs, it's hardly surprising that resentment has been growing against the rating agencies over the last few years. In January 2012, even the ECB governor Mario Draghi voiced the hope that 'we will learn to live without rating agencies'. However, this will remain wishful thinking until the reason that we can't do without rating agencies is recognized.

The reason is simple: once again, it's a matter of liquidity. The transformation of the debtor–creditor relationship into a negotiable bond entails the need for the bond to be assessed. If we want to learn to live without rating agencies, we must learn to live without financial markets.

In the Hoarding Business

Just like the big banks, big firms also accumulate liquidity. By the end of September 2011, the US non-financial firms held reserves amounting to US$1,730 billion in ready money, accounting for 6 per cent of their assets – the highest percentage since the post-war period. The ready money held by US firms has increased by 50 per cent over the pre-crisis levels. Apple alone holds liquidity for nearly one hundred billion dollars, equal to the market capitalization of McDonald's or the GDP of Slovakia.[37]

Europe's firms show a similar propensity: the 400 largest non-financial firms, according to the Bloomberg classification, hold 609 billion euros in ready money. It's the big firms that show the greatest propensity to hoard: half that sum is in the hands of the top thirty-five.[38] We also see firms that had committed to very different forms of investment playing the same game. In a recent interview, Marchionne stated that Fiat held ready money to the tune of 20 billion euros, justifying it with the fear of possible credit restrictions by the banks.[39]

So the firms prefer saving to investing because they fear losses. In doing so, they depress demand, private and public alike, for investment and consumption goods, driving families and public administrations to borrow yet more. Consequently, they eventually bring on the losses they wanted to avoid.

Much the same applies to family savings (when there are any). In times of depression, like the present, those who opt for the prudent and provident approach, putting aside part of their income for the harder times to come, are in practice, and despite themselves, helping to bring on the harder times.

It's a new, simple and linear version of the saving paradox illustrated by Keynes with the parable of the bananas. A community produces and consumes nothing but bananas. The workers do not spend all their income on bananas. A part is saved. And this part is equivalent to the investments in extending and developing cultivation. Now, what would happen if a campaign to incentivize saving was launched? There would be an increase in the amount of money saved, but there could be no counting on a comparable increase in the money invested in new plantations. In fact, there's a good chance that the entrepreneurs might refuse to invest, lest increased production should bring prices down, or for technical considerations, given the time it would take to set up new machinery or train new workers. On the other hand, there would be no change in the quantity of bananas put on the market: producers would aim at selling them all because bananas don't keep long. Therefore, since the quantity of money available to buy bananas would have decreased as a consequence of the campaign to promote saving, their price would have to decrease correspondingly. Apparently, the workers would benefit, being able to save even as they continue to buy the same amount of bananas at a lower price. However, the workers' savings would correspond to a net loss for the entrepreneurs, who would have made less on the sale of their bananas. The saving would not have increased the wealth of the community as a whole, measured in terms of bananas. Indeed, faced with losses, the entrepreneurs would have to reduce either the wages or the number of employees. But this in turn, as long as the campaign to promote saving went on, would only reduce spending on bananas yet further and the entrepreneurs would see their receipts dwindling. Any bankruptcies that might occur would actually lead to a loss in the overall wealth of the community in terms of bananas produced.

The conclusion is clear: saving money adds nothing to the wealth of an economy since the only possible increase in wealth comes from investing the saved money. Indeed, in so far as monetary saving exceeds real investment, the effective wealth may actually be diminished. Saving merely produces redistribution of income from the entrepreneurs to the savers: the gains of the latter correspond to the losses of the former, and could entail a fall in production.

Keynes returned to the point in more succinct but no less incisive terms in a letter to the governor of the Bank of England, dated 22 May 1930:

> For reasons which are too long and complicated to explain here, if our total investment (home plus foreign) is less than the amount of our current savings (i.e. that part of their incomes which individuals do not spend on consumption), then – in my opinion – it is absolutely certain that business losses and unemployment must ensue. This, of course, is a difficult theoretical proposition. It is very important that a competent decision should be reached on whether it is true or false. I can only say that I am ready to have my head chopped off if it is false![40]

The Liquidity Trap

Just a few months later, there was no longer any need to resort to tropical fables or acid tests for a compelling demonstration of the harm that could come from the rhetoric of saving. It was enough to outline the economic prospects for 1932. This was the title and subject matter of a lecture given by Keynes in Hamburg on 6 January 1932, in which accumulation of money was identified as the main cause of the crisis.

> The immediate causes of the financial panic – for that is what it is – are obvious. They are to be found in a catastrophic fall in the money value, not only of commodities, but of practically every kind of asset – a fall which has proceeded to a point at which the assets, held against money debts of every kind including bank deposits, no longer have a realisable value in money equal to the amount of the debt. We are now in the phase where the risk of carrying assets with borrowed money is so great that there is a competitive panic to get liquid. And each individual who succeeds in getting more liquid forces down the price of assets in the process of getting liquid, with the result that the margins of other individuals are impaired and their courage undermined. And so the process continues. [...] The competitive struggle for liquidity has now extended beyond individuals and institutions to nations and to governments.[41]

The economic effects of saving money emerge to the full in conditions of crisis, and notably of liquidity crisis, as the crisis we are still going through is called. The crisis makes clear the economic evils deriving from saving money: whenever doubts arise that certain forms of financial assets – for example, investments in shares, real estate, emerging markets or structured finance instruments – are likely to lose value, investors will prefer to sell them and hold their assets in the form of ready cash rather than run the risk of depreciation, at least in nominal terms. And yet the sale itself of such assets brings on their depreciation and the losses feared become the reality. In turn, this will further feed bearish expectations and swell the wave of sales yet more.

Thus, all at once money appears to be the only safe form of wealth, and it is saved at the expense of all investment. The demand is for money, and money alone. The entire economic system is turned upside down: competition in production turns into a 'competitive struggle for liquidity'. Everyone tries to spend less than they have coming in: firms, families, governments, states...to pay old debts, to pile up liquid reserves, because there's no trusting others, no confidence in the future.

2012 just like 1932: not exactly the prelude to a happy upturn. We've fallen into the liquidity trap again. And the central banks can go on flooding the economy with liquidity: it will only stagnate. Those that have it take good care not to lend it; those who lack it take equally good care not to borrow it – and all are bogged down.

Japan holds a lesson for Europe; its past could be our future. We are well on the way to depression. Like Japan, Europe is bound for its 'lost decade', with zero growth, if it does nothing about it. That is, zero if all goes well. Japan avoided a fall in GDP thanks only to an expansion in public spending. We may hope to do likewise, provided that we are ready to let our public debts grow, as did Japan, to over 200 per cent of GDP. But we aren't. In particular, creditors aren't prepared to provide the financing – especially if we persist in seeking our creditors abroad. So we are headed for a decade of depression: not zero growth, but negative growth.[42] Unless, that is, we invent some new forms of borrowing that don't depend on international capital markets, and new forms of money that don't have the intrinsic tendency to stagnate. Once again, it's a matter of depriving finance and money of their liquidity, to move on from capitalism to the market.

The Creeping Risk of Inflation

On the other hand, the present situation does not have a clear and univocal interpretation in terms of price dynamics. While it is true, as we have seen, that there are strong deflationary trends due to money withheld, accumulated and removed from circulation, the fact remains that the central banks have injected massive doses of it over the last five years.

For more than six years, since the year 2000, the inflation rate held extraordinarily steady in the eurozone at between 2% and 2.5%. Then it doubled, from 2% to 4%, when the

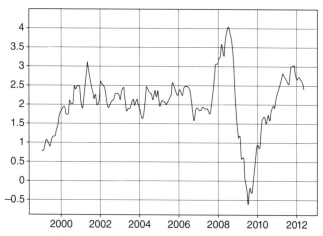

Figure 2.5 Inflation in the eurozone (Harmonised Index of Consumer Prices)
Source: European Central Bank, Statistical Data Warehouse (http:sdw
.ecb.int)

sub-prime crisis broke out between the summers of 2007 and 2008. When the crisis hit the banks with the Lehman crash in September 2008, inflation plunged below zero, and for a few months at the end of 2009 the eurozone experienced deflation. Then the inflation rate began rising once again. Today, it's back to normal levels (Figure 2.5). But for how long?

The determinants of fluctuations in inflation are to be sought on the supply side, not the demand side. The rise in prices is due to rising costs, and in particular fuel costs. The most significant historical analogy is with the oil shock of the 1970s. It was oil prices that pushed up consumer prices. But, today as then, it is the increase in money supply rather than economic recovery that drives up oil prices. (And, today as then, the political reasons associated with tensions in the Middle East are purely contingent.) A decisive part in driving up oil prices was played by the expansionary monetary policies implemented by major western central banks.

The price of oil is rising, but what's behind the rise? It's certainly not attributable to a recovery in production and so in the demand for fuel to produce goods and transport them to the various markets. Recession is persisting in the advanced countries while a slow-down is threatening emerging countries, too. One might, then, be tempted to ascribe the increase to issues on the supply side and indeed there are various reasons to fear a reduction in the quantity of oil available on the international markets – in particular, the embargo against Iran, and that country's threat to block the Strait of Hormuz. And yet today, as in the 1970s, geopolitical tensions can at most act as a trigger for a burst of inflation: then as now, the explosive charge comes from the enormous mass of liquidity put into circulation by the central banks.

It is monetary expansion that lies behind the rising prices of raw materials and agricultural produce, and not just oil. In times of uncertainty, when any investment risks losing value, whether in property, shares or even sovereign bonds, raw materials might seem the safest refuge to entrust wealth to. When money seeking investment starts running after commodities available only in limited quantities and not readily reproducible, the prices of the latter inevitably start rising. In other words, inflation is generated.

The lesson is there in Goethe's *Faust*, when Mephistopheles, dressed as the court jester, encourages the emperor to print paper money. The emperor prints his banknotes with no backing and the jester rushes off to spend them, seeking the safety of real commodities. Those who fear inflation help to generate it, to the point, potentially, of hyperinflation.

It would be simpler to admit that central banks have now lost control of the quantity of money. In fact, the quantity of money effectively circulating depends far more on the behaviour of the eventual users than on the decisions of the generators. We'll take as good the quantity equation because it gives us an accounting identity: $MV = PT$, the quantity of money (M) multiplied by its velocity of circulation (V) is equal to the price level (P) multiplied by the volume of transactions (T). However, we have to recognize that the trend in P depends much more on the unforeseeable variations in V, and thus on the behaviour of the holders of money, than on the deliberate changes of M, or in other words on the strategies of the central bank.

The Decline of the Dollar?

Just as each central bank creates money for its national economy, so the United States creates money for the world economy. Since 1971, we have been in an international 'fiat money' regime. Since then, the United States has poured enormous quantities of dollars into the world economy through its balance of payments deficit, creating a dollar inflation such as could jeopardize the role of the dollar as global currency.

For sixty years, the dollar has been officially performing the function of international medium of payment and reserve. The pound had served the same purpose over the preceding seventy years, coping with ups and downs. And there are further analogies between the dollar and pound that make interesting comparison:

- both qualified as reserve currencies in virtue of their gold convertibility;
- both the United Kingdom and the United States began as creditors and ended as debtors;
- both have maintained pre-eminence in finance, having lost it at the industrial level.

However, at least at first sight, the analogies seem to stop here. For various reasons, the dollar appears to be able to keep a good hold on its position as international currency:

- the dollar continues to be used as an international means of payment and also for the purchase of goods that do not come from the United States;
- over 60 per cent of the world's official reserves are denominated in dollars, and the percentage has shown virtually no change over the last fifteen years (Figure 2.6);

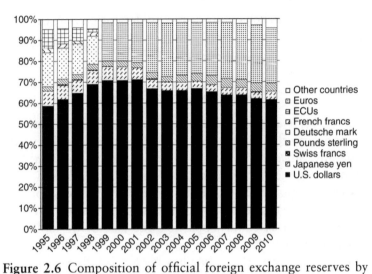

Figure 2.6 Composition of official foreign exchange reserves by currency
Source: International Monetary Fund, Currency Composition of Official Foreign Exchange Reserves (COFER)

- the markets for financial assets denominated in dollars are the most liquid in the world;
- evidencing the high international demand for dollars, the exchange rate has depreciated only gradually over the last ten years, still holding even after the crisis broke out, despite high and persistent US balance-of-payments deficits: the present level of the real effective exchange rate remains fairly close to the 1973 level, when the floating exchange rate system came in;
- finally, US debt securities have also continued to enjoy strong demand and a reduction in yield, despite the ills the crisis has inflicted on the US budget.

On the other hand, there are at least as many signs suggesting a possible future decline in the dollar as international currency:

- to some extent, it has already given way to other currencies in payment and reserve functions;

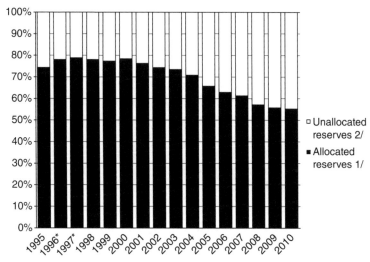

Figure 2.7 Growth in unidentified foreign exchange reserves
Note: [white] Foreign exchange reserves in an unidentified currency;
[black] Foreign exchange reserves in an identified currency
Source: International Monetary Fund, Currency Composition of Official
Foreign Exchange Reserves (COFER)

- over the last ten years, the proportion of reserves of unknown denomination has almost doubled (Figure 2.7);
- above all, the US balance of trade has for thirty-five years been showing a deficit that has by now become chronic.

Now, the only condition that can ultimately ensure stability for a currency over time is equilibrium in the issuing country's balance of trade.

With a free-floating system, the exchange rate is a price and, like all prices, it depends on the demand vis-à-vis the supply. In turn, the international demand for a currency depends upon its utilization to finance international trade and investments. And ultimately, as we have seen, the latter can only be temporary flows, destined to reverse when the time comes round for the debt to be paid back. Thus the only real demand for a country's currency corresponds to the demand for commodities from that country (net of the flow of commodities in the other direction). Whenever, thanks to some convention, agreement, deliberate intervention or simple expectation, the exchange rate is held artificially at a level other than that which ensures equilibrium in the balance of trade, it is bound sooner or later to undergo adjustment. The extent and abruptness of the adjustment will correspond to the degree of imbalance that has developed with an exchange rate shifted out of alignment with equilibrium conditions.

The Lesson Offered by the Pound

Until a few months before the beginning of the First World War, the sterling standard enjoyed a certain stability. This was possible because the United Kingdom was a creditor country and because it shouldered a good part of the burden of adjusting potential imbalances, in particular by raising the interest rate whenever flights of capital threatened.

Similarly, the dollar standard enjoyed a fair degree of stability after the Second World War, as long as the United States was a creditor country and bore the cost of post-war reconstruction and the Cold War, offering Europe loans at facilitated rates or non-repayable aid and granting it the benefit of favourable exchange rates.

By contrast, after the war, and as a consequence of it, the United Kingdom had become a debtor country with a weak currency. Nevertheless, it wanted to restore gold convertibility at the pre-war parity. This was, however, an unrealistic level, unrelated to the country's effective competitiveness and therefore a source of imbalances. The overvalued exchange rate led to a chronic balance-of-payments deficit for the United Kingdom and generated powerful deflationary pressure on its entire economy until the country had no choice but to abandon anchorage on gold.

Bearing the burden of aid and the Cold War, the United States soon found itself a country in deficit, too, losing in competitiveness and eventually forced to put an end to gold convertibility in order to devalue the currency. Unlike the pound, however, the dollar didn't lose its international reserve function when the foundation of its legitimacy – the gold base – was demolished. There were two reasons for this surprising outcome. Firstly, there was no alternative: in 1971 there was no one to take over the gold baton in relay, and so the United States had to keep running with a paper baton. And secondly, dollars had now found an outlet in the increasingly liberalized, globalized, deep and liquid capital markets. Liquidity took the place of convertibility as the – by no means solid – foundation of the international monetary system.

The Rate of Change

The transition from pound to dollar could be steered fairly smoothly in virtue of the fact that these were the currencies of two allied countries and that, moreover, the United Kingdom could still count on the use of its currency by the colonies and Commonwealth countries.

On the other hand, the slow decline of the dollar was softened by the simple lack of any alternative – and the lack was rendered 'sustainable', thanks to the growth of the financial markets and international capital movements. Inevitably, however, all this only contributed to generating imbalance upon imbalance, eventually proving unsustainable.

The utilization of the dollar as reserve currency reflects, and indeed entails, the growth of the United States's net foreign debt (Figure 2.8). It also provides it with support, but how long can it last?

The flow of international investments to the United States finds no justification in their yield, which is consistently lower than the yield of US foreign investments. The United States earns a liquidity premium: thanks to the higher liquidity of its markets, it can pay its (public and private) debts at a lower rate than any other country. And thanks to this advantage, the country is able earn a rent on its own debts

Figure 2.8 'Our debt is your money': net international debts of US and official reserves (millions of dollars)
Source: IMF Statistics Department COFER Database and International Financial Statistics

– an 'exorbitant privilege' which is, however, also showing ever more clearly its cost: namely, that of being at the mercy of its creditors. It is hardly surprising if an empire like China, with thousands of years behind it, hesitates to take over the ill-omened baton.

The great risk is that abandonment of the dollar as reserve currency could lead to an abrupt appreciation, setting off a series of competitive devaluations. And there's always the chance that currency wars may develop into trade wars or even (God forbid, as our grandparents used to say) wars *tout court*.

Without dwelling on cataclysmic possible outcomes, the most immediate economic upshot could well be a drastic rise in inflation. The major central banks, with the Fed on the front line, have created enormous quantities of money over the last five years to contain the crisis, avoid bankruptcies, shore up the banks' balance sheets and revitalize investment. It is widely believed that until there are signs of recovery, this great mass of liquidity cannot translate into higher prices.

We cannot share this optimism. Even without contributing in the least to reviving consumption, the money generously made available by the central banks could drive up the prices of financial or property assets, creating new bubbles, or could fuel speculation on the raw material markets, generating cost inflation every bit as bad as that experienced in the 1970s.

Actually, that decade constitutes a historical precedent that must not be forgotten or misinterpreted. The oil crises were obviously triggered by factors causing instability in the Middle East (and, from Sudan to Iran, such factors are not lacking today), but fuelling the inflationary flare-ups was the international plethora of dollars no longer anchored to gold. A similar risk exists today: if demand for the dollar as reserve currency were to fall, it would come in for devaluation in real terms even before devaluation with respect to other currencies. Commodities could take over from the dollar as a store of value. And perhaps they have already started to.

The Rise of the Yuan

The yuan is the most obvious candidate to replace the dollar. China is the country with the greatest capacity in the world for export, and there is potential demand for the yuan, for transactions if nothing else. Indeed, many countries have already begun to hold reserves in yuan, mainly China's trading partners, not just in Asia but also in Africa and in emerging countries. China has announced its intention to increase the liquidity of its capital markets and has already begun to do so.

A significant sign is the growth in assets denominated in yuan abroad. Just as the Eurodollar market developed in London in the 1960s, so today a 'euroyuan' market is developing, again in London. Yuan circulating outside China are designated different initials (CNH) from those given to yuan circulating in China (CNY).

A good part of yuan transactions outside China takes place on the Hong Kong market. Here, the total volume of deposits rose fivefold between mid-2010 and mid-2011, rising from less than 110 billion CNH (corresponding to about 10 billion euros) to over 550 billion CNH (50 billion euros).

What made the surge possible was a slackening of control over monetary movements connected with commercial operations. It came to a halt at the end of 2011 with an increase in the issue of bonds denominated in yuan (known as 'Dim Sum' bonds) and sold on the world market, offering investors interested in holding assets in yuan a more remunerative alternative to deposit.[43] The global market for bonds denominated in yuan increased threefold in 2011, reaching an exchange value of US$16.8 billion according to the Hong Kong monetary authority[44] (Figure 2.9).

Such growth also seems to have been encouraged by an active policy on the part of the Chinese government.[45] China's efforts to turn the yuan into an international currency have accelerated in recent months.[46]

At the same time, the rise of the yuan as international currency is also being favoured by equally active policies on the part of public authorities and financial operators in the

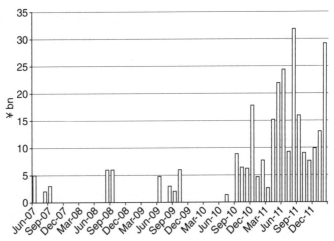

Figure 2.9 Offshore Chinese bond issuance (in yuan)
Source: The City of London Corporation

West. The City of London has formed a working group involving the participation of the British Treasury, the Bank of England, the Financial Services Authority and five of the major private banks, with strong representation in both London and Hong Kong. The aim is to underpin the growth of assets in yuan. The UK Chancellor of the Exchequer George Osborne has guaranteed 'the strong support of the Government'.[47] Similar ventures have been launched by Singapore and Tokyo.

London is pursuing its interests, aiming to become 'the leading western hub for RMB business'.[48] In fact, in the United Kingdom the financial sector constitutes the most dynamic sector of the economy: it contributes to the gross domestic product to the tune of nearly 10 per cent (more than in any other country in the world) and, even more significantly for UK exports, helping at least to a certain extent to lighten the balance of trade deficit.

We should, however, be wondering whether the rise of the yuan as international currency is really in the interests of the West and of the rest of the world. China is not a country in equilibrium. Its systematic balance-of-trade surplus simply reflects the need to shuffle off its internal imbalances elsewhere. China needs to export in order to grow and needs to grow in order to maintain social peace. On the other hand, the accumulation of surplus only aggravates inflationary pressures, together with the risk of real-estate bubbles, over-investment and the consequent further increase in productive capacity, well beyond any possibility of being absorbed through domestic demand. In this state of affairs, foreign investment affords an outlet, currency swaps constituting one form, while the accumulation of yuan reserves by the beneficiary countries is a corollary. The risk is that China, like the United States before, may find itself going from a surplus to a deficit without ever attaining a balance.

To all intents and purposes, the euro would be a more credible candidate if it didn't risk remaining a victim of its internal imbalances, for at least the eurozone balance of payments is in equilibrium with the rest of the world. In any case, even starting from a situation of equilibrium, the use of a national currency as international currency is in itself bound to generate imbalances. It happened with the dollar, as Robert Triffin had foreseen as early as 1960, when he voiced the dilemma that bears his name. What the dilemma amounts to is: on the one hand, to continue favouring global economic growth, the country supplying international currency must continue to create it through a balance-of-payments deficit. On the other hand, however, to keep the international currency stable in relation to the other currencies, the country providing it must keep its external accounts balanced. If dilemmas are articulated, it's not simply for the sake of doing so but, as Triffin knew full well, to avoid getting caught out by them.

International Currency Needed

Significantly, the idea of using an international currency, such as the special drawing rights (SDRs), and not a national currency as international reserve asset had been advocated in March 2009 by the governor of the People's Bank of China. Zhou Xiaochuan had singled out the major factor of imbalance in adopting a national currency as the international one, and he described the implications in precisely the terms of the 'Triffin dilemma'.

In keeping with his analysis, he proposed the institution of a fully international currency on the model of the bancor recommended by Keynes at Bretton Woods. Alas, the proposal was swept aside, having never been given serious consideration.

What exactly did the international monetary system reform urged by Keynes consist of? We have recently collected in one volume passages in which Keynes himself illustrated and advocated his plan, together with the proposal by Zhou Xiaochuan, who uses it as an example, and a series of texts demonstrating the relevance of the underlying principles.[49] Here we will simply outline the essential characteristics.

Keynes proposed the institution of an international clearing house called the Clearing Union. The primary function of this institution was to finance international trade, allowing for temporary imbalances in individual countries' balances of trade, but ensuring that they indeed be temporary. In other words, the aim was to guarantee countries the greatest possible freedom in trade but at the same time to maintain a trend towards equilibrium in each of the countries' external accounts, achieving compatibility between freedom and equilibrium in international trade. On the one hand, it's a matter of favouring international trade in respect of the principle of international division of labour, by virtue of which each country is able to contribute both to its own well-being and to that of all the others, concentrating on what it is best able to do. At the same time, it's a way to ensure that each country always tends back towards equilibrium, selling commodities for a value equivalent to the commodities it receives in exchange – so avoiding the type of situation in which some countries specialize in producing debts and others in accumulating credits and reserves, generating persistent imbalances.

To finance international trade, the Clearing Union was to provide each member country with a current account denominated in an international currency, distinct from the national currencies, called the bancor. The name itself suggests an analogy between the functioning of the Clearing Union and that of a normal bank: the countries use their current accounts with the Clearing Union to pay for goods and services which they purchase from other countries. Thus, for example, if country A imports from country B to a value of 100 bancor, B will then have a credit of 100 and A a debit of 100 on their respective accounts. However, the analogy goes no further. In fact, the Clearing Union is endowed with a series of characteristics that distinguish it from a normal bank and make it a clearing house or, to be precise, an institution in which credits and debits are not made to be accumulated but, rather, to be reciprocally offset.

To begin with, in the Clearing Union there are no deposits nor capital, nor indeed reserves. Countries need pay nothing into their accounts. This means that all accounts are opened with an initial zero balance. Trade is financed, each country being granted an overdraft facility, or in other words the possibility to go into the red up to a certain set figure. This means that each country is set a quota proportional to the volume of its foreign trade which determines the limit not only on its negative balance, but also, symmetrically, on its positive balance.

Here, then, we have the second difference from a normal bank. In the Clearing Union creditors and debtors are the object of perfectly symmetrical treatment. The limit set on the borrowing of each country also applies as the ceiling on its credit: no credits can be accumulated above a certain threshold because, in so doing, contractional pressure would be brought to bear on international trade. Thus the Clearing Union embodies the principle that, in international trade, it is obligatory to pay one's debts; however, there is also the perfectly matching obligation to spend one's credits. And the more the creditors are induced to spend their credits, the easier it will prove for the debtors to pay their debts.

To further ease debtors and creditors back to the equilibrium position, corresponding to a zero current account balance, Keynes brought in a further symmetry which distinguishes the Clearing Union mechanism even more strikingly from the functioning of a normal bank. In the Clearing Union, as in a normal bank, the debtors pay interest on their negative balances. This serves to cover the costs of running the payment system and to incentivize debtors to settle their debts. Unlike the procedure in a normal bank, however, in the Clearing Union creditors, too, have to pay interest on their assets; thus they, too, are incentivized to get their account back in balance. The fact that the creditors also have to pay is justified from a systemic point of view since it powers convergence to equilibrium, but it is also justified within the particular perspective of each individual creditor country. In fact, unlike the creditor of a bank, the creditor country does not need to be remunerated, for it has not paid anything into its account, but simply sold commodities. Like the debtor, it has benefited from the existence of the clearing system: just as the Clearing Union enables the debtor country to purchase what it could not otherwise have afforded, so it also enables the creditor country to sell what it could not otherwise have sold. The 'interest' paid by creditors is the price they have to pay to enjoy the benefits of clearing.

Should the symmetrical incentives to return to equilibrium prove insufficient to prevent the formation of persistent imbalances, Keynes's project included the rider that adjustment could be eased with appropriate adjustments of the exchange rate. A country in deficit could, and in particular circumstances would have to, adjust its exchange rate downwards vis-à-vis the bancor in order to regain competitiveness while, again symmetrically, a country in surplus could, and in some cases would have to, make upward adjustment.

Without going into further detail, it should by now be clear that adoption of such a system could afford significant benefits today in the face of the persistent imbalances shaking the world economy. More decisive efforts need to be made in this direction. An international currency associated with a clearing system remains today the only scheme that could reconcile growth and freedom in international trade with the imperative to avoid chronic accumulation of global imbalances by ensuring that all money is spent and all debts are paid.

3

The European Crisis and the Need for a New European Payments Union

'Being at one is god-like and good, but human, too human, the mania Which insists there is only the One, one country, one truth [and one currency].'

F. Hölderlin, *The Root of All Evil*[1]

The crisis in Europe, too, is a money matter. Sovereign debts are but the secondary symptoms of a problem whose roots lie in the flaws in the construction of the single currency. Finding a way out from the crisis means reforming the monetary union. The euro is on the brink of a precipice, with a real risk of falling and smashing itself to pieces. The ailing countries' plans for recovery may not yield the desired results. Even without evoking prospects of default, the depreciation of government bonds means huge losses for the banks holding them, which face inexorable downgrading by the rating agencies. In the meantime, rising interest rates, the banks' dire straits and the governments' austerity measures combine to depress aggregate demand and thwart recovery, feeble as it is, throughout the continent, including Germany.

In turn, the depression is fuelling social and political tensions. The workers in the debtor countries, labouring under increasing fiscal pressure and welfare cuts, react with violent indignation and industrial action against the oppression of the policies imposed by international creditors. The workers in creditor countries, who are more productive, receive wages that do not match their productivity and retire later, wax indignant and protest against compensation for the wastefulness of others. On either side, government leaders are incapable of thrashing out and implementing a coherent and practicable solution in concert and in command of the issues. In reality, they are not leaders but followers, as has been aptly observed: they latch onto dominant populism and nationalism in an attempt to curry voters' favour and sit tight, but their seats are wobbling dangerously under them.

At the same time, the signs of increasingly widespread nationalistic feelings are all too evident. In recent elections, the xenophobic parties of the right have gained support from northern Europe to Greece, where the Golden Dawn MPs pummel their political opponents on television. A German colleague of ours who took the liberty of pointing out – at an academic conference – the responsibility of her government in the euro crisis and Germany's interest in avoiding it was sent an overtly anti-Semitic threatening letter. Not so long ago, the Dutch minister of finance proposed granting credits to Greece only with an adequate pledge of state-owned property (the Parthenon, presumably) as collateral. A comparably punitive approach was adopted by the Reparations Commission in the 1920s, spelling doom for the Weimar Republic, left to populist revanchism and finally Nazism.[2]

The atmosphere in Europe is increasingly reminiscent of the storm clouds that hung over the early decades of the twentieth century. Having set out to construct European political union on economic integration, and the latter on monetary union, disintegration of the euro could undermine the entire European project, leaving the field open once again to the possibility of war. After one century, we could witness yet another 'suicide of Europe'.

Neocolonialism Strikes Back

And this time the United States won't save us. We might look to China – but that's very different. Through the pages of the *Financial Times*, the American economist Barry Eichengreen called on Europe to recognize its insufficiency and invoke the celestial intervention of the Celestial Empire. The mandarinate is a Chinese institution, mandarinism a certain spirit...

It's rumoured that one of Italy's past treasury ministers negotiated the sale of part of the country's sovereign debt to a Chinese sovereign fund, while his successor, as soon as he was in office, set out on what he himself called a 'roadshow', which is generally taken to refer to the activity of financial promoters hunting down new investors. If the economic advantage of this sort of marketing is clear, its political cost is enormous. At stake – in a progression that is as insidious as it is gradual and imperceptible – is the very sovereignty of the nation. A few years ago, the former minister Giulio Tremonti warned against the possibility of 'colonialism striking back'. With the help of various ministers past and present, nemesis has struck.

At a conference on the reform of global governance a few months ago, commenting on our graph illustrating credits granted by China to the West, a Chinese diplomat warned us in impeccable American English: 'there's no such thing as a free lunch.' This is not only the title of the book published by Milton Friedman in 1975, but also the motto that became the leitmotif of the extension of the market on a global scale over the last forty years under the aegis of neoliberal doctrine. Paradoxically, it is in fact the Americans who've been able to enjoy free meals on that market, paying with pieces of paper worth, if not nothing, at any rate something that remains to be seen.

Today, the hegemon's apprentice has learnt the lesson and brought the bill. China no longer intends to go on accumulating dollars and treasury bonds, and has begun to dispose of them in order to buy real goods, raw materials, infrastructures: ports, from Greece to Estonia, motorways, from Germany to Turkey. And then there are industrial investments, strategic alliances...But this is precisely what we have been doing in the West for a couple of centuries: it's called imperialistic colonization, and 'they' weren't too happy about it...

On top of this, we have the structural reforms which the countries of Europe are inflicting upon themselves. They are supposed to relaunch economic growth. They were tried out in ex-colonies in the past, and now they are being implemented in Europe, too, much like the experimental reform of human beings by imperialist 'civilizers' in Africa between the nineteenth and twentieth century, subsequently implemented at home in totalitarian regimes.

The Age of Austerity

It's a murky picture, and the way it's described by the authorities who should be indicating a way out hardly makes it any clearer. Actually, the recommendations offered by the political authorities and experts sound more like millenarian sermons. Interpreting its role as virtuous country, Germany has formulated its call for penance and self-mortification: prepare, oh ye debtors, for self-denial and sacrifice and you will be granted perpetual indulgence in return for your temporary suffering. Again and again, financial breviary insists on the same spiritual exercises: repent, apparel yourselves in sackcloth, cover your heads in ashes and rest your hopes in the magnanimity of the Supreme Judge...

So what is the point of the austerity measures brought in with the new European Fiscal Compact? According to the politicians who favoured them, they serve to reassure the ECB and induce it to buy the member countries' sovereign bonds as well as, more generally, undertaking an even more expansionary monetary policy. The ECB's version, on the other hand, is that they serve to keep the markets happy and so bring down interest rates. As for market dealers, they see them as serving no better purpose than to jeopardize yet further the solvency of public and private debtors.[3]

Given the present form of economic institutions, the only policy allowed is the policy deemed appropriate by the financial market, regardless of its content. So what does the market want? Nothing clear or definite. Actually, it doesn't really know; it's just afraid of dying and needs reassurance.

Our governments' measures may be appropriate and practical, or they may be senseless and counterproductive, but in any case if the market deems them appropriate it will begin to buy our bonds once again, the yield will fall and we'll be saved. Like the totalitarian autocrat described by Arthur Koestler in that memorable novel *Darkness at Noon*, the market is always right provided its word is never doubted, even if it should constantly proclaim new versions of the truth.

Are Eurobonds a Solution?

In May 2010, under the presidency of Jean-Claude Trichet, the ECB brought in the Securities Markets Programme to allay tensions. The idea was that, departing from its statutory constraints, the ECB could buy member countries' public debt securities on condition that purchase be made on the secondary market and not directly from the debtor country. Trichet justified this dispensation as a measure necessary to correct the errors of the market, or in other words the prices of government bonds not in line with fundamentals: this ECB corrective intervention would be called for in cases of deviation that risked getting in the way of monetary policy. As a result of the programme operations, the ECB now holds 214 billion euros in eurozone government bonds.[4]

The expediency of extending recourse to such measures is still the object of heated debate among the ECB Executive Board. Germany, of course, is against it, concerned that ECB purchase of government bonds could turn into unqualified support for the more thriftless governments with a consequent inflationary trend.

This is, apparently, simply a new front opened in an old war being fought in the field of monetary geopolitics, where the German hawks clash with the doves of the rest of Europe. One might also be tempted to see in this a deeper ideological conflict, one side holding that the market should have the last word while the other side attributes the final say to the political sphere, even when it's a matter of assessing a state's creditworthiness. Where does the ultimate truth lie – with the market or with the central bank?

In support of the market view, we have the international accounting standards, according to which even government bonds should be entered into the balance sheet at 'fair value', i.e., the current market value, in accordance with the 'market-to-market' principle. The European Banking Authority (EBA) also recommends following this principle. But it's a debatable principle, and dangerous to boot. Not only is there a risk of financial markets' solvency evaluations departing from the fundamentals, but they could even shape the course of things: if the markets expect a state's default, they could eventually bring it on, despite all efforts made for recovery, driving interest rates on the debt up to unsustainable levels.[5] Unreserved adoption of the 'fair value' principle could lead to a reversal in the relationship between finance and reality: it would be expectations that shaped the course of events, and not vice versa.

On the other hand, entrusting the central bank with the faculty to intervene in the government bond market to correct any misalignments that might occur with the fundamentals introduces an equally dangerous exception system. What 'fundamentals' are to be taken into account to evaluate a sovereign state's solvency? What are the criteria to measure misalignment? In practice, it would mean depriving the market of the faculty to decide on the default or rescue of a state, to attribute it to the central bank. In purchasing government bonds, the central bank acts as lender of last resort.

The lender of last resort is like the judge of last appeal, having the last word.

The possibility for the ECB to take on the function of lender of last resort is usually associated with the unification of economic policies at the European level. Fiscal unification of the eurozone countries is the essential precondition to replace the individual states' public debt securities with debt securities issued by the Union itself – Eurobonds, as they are called. In turn, the issue of Eurobonds is commonly seen as a necessary condition for the ECB to be able to buy sovereign debt securities without being faced with the problem of having to decide to buy the securities of this or that country, which risks favouring the more thriftless and irresponsible.

However, we cannot join in the increasingly widespread consensus to move in this direction. Of course, fiscal union and the issue of Eurobonds would open the way for the eurozone to exit from the impasse, making sovereign debts more sustainable and opening a source of financing to implement those expansionary policies that all now see as indispensable. In other words, on the strength of such a set of measures, the ECB would be able to operate exactly like the Fed. At best, however, it would be a temporary palliative. There would, of course, be the advantage of putting Europe on a par with the United States, the United Kingdom and all the countries able to finance their public debt by printing money. At the same time, however, it would have the daunting flaw of accurately moulding Europe on a model that, through an unlimited increase of liquidity, created the conditions for the present crisis to break out.[6]

Moreover, there is scant chance of a European political union proving truly successful and achieving real solidity if it is driven by financial urgency. Many see the completion of political union as the only way out of an impasse where an either/or is becoming ever more imperative: either strengthen the Union or break it up. But can the political union, heralded for decades and never accomplished, really be achieved under the threat of breakdown? Actually, such compacting under pressure – already anticipated with the 'fiscal compact', moreover – could in fact further aggravate the centrifugal, disruptive pressures accumulating as the nationalist and Eurosceptic parties ride from strength to strength. Paradoxically, the approach being taken to achieve union could accelerate disintegration. To reconcile political long-sightedness with the urgency of the situation, very different methods are called for.

The Wrong Diagnosis

Actually, the determination to unify Europe along these lines, blazoning rigour and trampling autonomies, is unjustified. Indeed, such recommendations reflect a viewpoint that is as misconceived as it is widespread and firmly rooted. If we can only throw off the blinkers that prevent us from appraising the problem in the right terms, then we can begin to see that a solution is not far away.

Two errors of perspective risk leading to the dissolution of the euro. First we must eliminate them, and then move on to the constructive stage. To begin with, despite the obsessive attention they have received from the very outset of the convergence process, it isn't public debts as such that constitute a problem for the endurance of monetary union. In so far as the public debt securities are in the hands of the citizens of the state that issues them, there is no need for foreigners to worry about them. In other words, a national public debt becomes an international problem only in so far as it is held abroad. The evidence is eloquent. The Japanese public debt has been able to exceed 220 per cent of GDP, no less, without causing alarm because it is largely financed by the savings of the Japanese themselves (Figure 3.1).

Counter-evidence is offered by Ireland, which has ended up among the PIIGS (Portugal, Ireland, Italy, Greece and Spain, the group of shaky economies), due to the huge foreign debts of its private banking system, although its public debt/GDP was amongst the lowest in Europe (about 25 per cent in 2007). The cause of Ireland's crisis lay in the over-indebtedness resulting from foreign capital attracted more

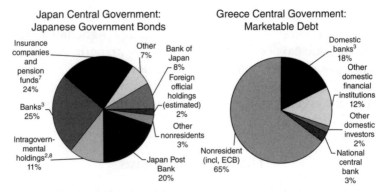

Figure 3.1 Who holds public debt?
Source: International Monetary Fund, *Fiscal Monitor September 2011: Addressing Fiscal Challenges to Reduce Economic Risks*, Washington, 2011

by tax concessions than by productive investments: the increase in the public debt (up to nearly 100 per cent of GDP) is the consequence of rescues necessitated in turn by the failure of a development model based on growth in financial assets. Ireland is one case, but an emblematic case, in a system in which states have run up debts to save those markets that now censure their overgrowth – like Aesop's travellers who criticize the fruitlessness of the plane tree whose shade they have enjoyed.

It is surely significant that, since the outbreak of the crisis, public debts have grown all over the world. And yet, as the data show, the growth has not been any more pronounced in the countries now in the eye of the storm. In fact, if we look at the dynamics of the debt/GDP ratio over the last ten years, Italy is among the more virtuous countries, while Greece is on an equal standing with Germany (Figure 3.2)!

Thus, the public debt must be dislodged from its position as the arbiter of Europe's fortunes, and for at least three reasons.

To begin with, it is certainly not the objective measure of good conduct that it is made out to be: as has been observed, the measurement criteria vary from one country to another

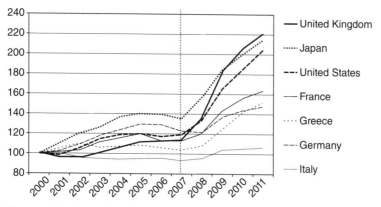

Figure 3.2 Growth of public debt/GDP ratio (index vr 2000 = 100)
Source: Authors' calculations based on the International Monetary Fund, World Economic Outlook, October 2010

and if, as elsewhere, the liabilities of the German loan and deposit bank (KfW) were included, entirely guaranteed by the state, Germany's public debt (which is already, in absolute terms, second globally only to that of the United States) would shoot up from 80 per cent to 100 per cent of GDP.

Secondly, the restrictive measures brought in to reduce public debt can only aggravate crisis, unemployment and social distress at a time when interest rates, at an all time low, should on the contrary be encouraging investment: is it possible that, to paraphrase Keynes at a more modest level, there is no infrastructure improvement in Europe that could promise returns even as low as 2 per cent? The good intention to reduce waste, corruption and tax evasion should not stop any state from making productive investments.

Lastly, leaving every member state free to decide when to borrow from its citizens, Europe should be worrying solely about that part of the public and private debts that is not financed by domestic saving. The proposal Giulio Tremonti made when he was minister to include private saving alongside public debt as a criterion of stability goes in the right direction but stops halfway. Why take the two variables

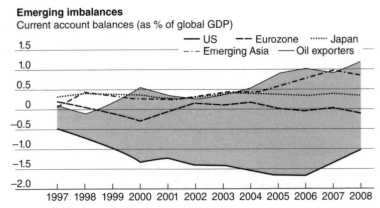

Emerging imbalances
Current account balances (as % of global GDP)

Figure 3.3 Global imbalances, European balance (current account balances as percentage of global GDP)
Source: International Monetary Fund

separately when what really counts is the difference between them? It's a matter of algebra: all that is needed to reform the stability pact is to consider the public debt net of private saving, i.e., the external debt.

Here, we come to our second consideration: the foreign debts we are now struggling to finance are debts between European countries, not with the rest of the world. It seems obvious, but evidently it isn't if foreign lenders, like the IMF or China, are continually being invoked, and if thoughts are even turning to the issue of Eurobonds for Europe to find financing on the world markets.

Whatever advocates of intervention in Europe by the IMF or China may say, however, the eurozone as a whole, unlike the United States, has no deficit in its external accounts, and so it has no need of other people's money (Figure 3.3).

This is all there is to the dramatic paradox of the European crisis, and we had better learn to see it for what it is: we are victims solely of our inability to grant one another credit reciprocally. In a pathological mood swing, we have gone from indiscriminate concession of credit at virtually zero rates to an equally indiscriminate clampdown at usurious rates. If the PIIGS are coming in for a beating today, it's

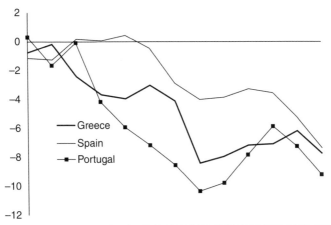

Figure 3.4 Countries in deficit (current account balances as percentage of GDP, 1993–2005)
Source: European Commission, *Quarterly Report on the Euro Area* 5(4) (2006)

because yesterday getting a loan was like stealing acorns from a blind pig!

When the crisis had yet to break out, a report by the European Commission had warned against possible risks deriving from persistent imbalances in eurozone current accounts. Particular reference was made to the deficits of Greece, Portugal and Spain which had been growing since the introduction of monetary union and by 2005 were already approaching 10 per cent of the respective GDPs in all three countries (Figure 3.4).

A significant risk factor pointed out by the Commission lay in the circumstance that these deficits were not covered by long-term loans but left to short-term financing; in other words, they were financed not through direct investments from abroad (which were actually negative in the case of Spain and Portugal), but through portfolio investments and bank loans. There had been an appreciable increase in bank loans from countries in surplus, and in particular from Germany. So who, or what, was to blame for these deficits?

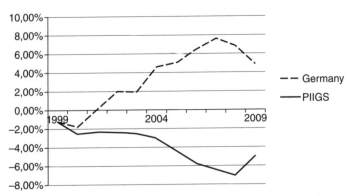

Figure 3.5 (Monetary) Union leads to (commercial) imbalance (current account balances as percentage of GDP)
Source: C. Altomonte and A. Villafranca, 'Not only Public Debt: Towards a New Pact on the Euro', ISPI Policy Brief, October 2010, p. 198

The Commission had no doubt: financing them had become that much easier thanks to the integration of Europe's financial markets, in turn made possible through monetary union.[7] Effectively, as from the constitution of monetary union, the gap between surplus countries and deficit countries only widened (Figure 3.5). This was no mere coincidence. In fact, by removing the exchange risk, the introduction of the euro opened the way for the countries of southern Europe to finance their current account deficits.

Must we conclude that today's Europe simply can't manage to discipline itself without having to resort to intervention from outside?

Signs of Easing Up?

Under pressure on all sides, Germany is in fact beginning to budge. The signs are coming thick and fast: suddenly the Bundesbank is taking an easier line on inflation ('we could accept a slightly higher rate in Germany, while the others work their way out of recession'), the minister of finance Schäuble opens up to the idea of higher wages to boost domestic demand (and help other eurozone countries), the CDU (Christian Democratic Union) appears ready to accept the minimum wage and Peter Altmaier, second-in-command in Merkel's party, is showing a cautiously positive attitude towards the Project Bonds (while rejection of Eurobonds remains inflexible).

The signs are all the more positive for being unexpected. So far, Germany had taken an uncompromising stance on defence against any manoeuvres that might have inflationary effects due, it is said, to an atavistic fear dating back to the hyperinflation of Weimar. This may well be the deep-rooted reason for Germany's inflation aversion, and there can be no denying that we must learn from history. But we must learn aright, and frankly even in the period between the two world wars there are, we feel, rather different lessons to learn. Traumatic as it was, the hyperinflation lasted just about two years, from 1921 to 1923. And it was settled almost instantly, as soon as the old devalued mark was replaced with the new Rentenmark, covered by the guarantee of land and industrial products. Far more dramatic was the deflation following upon the crisis of 1929 which lasted the whole of the following decade, infecting the entire world and contributing to creating the right economic and social conditions for the rise of Nazism.[8] Is it possible that even now, in Germany, in Europe and in the rest of the capitalist economies, the lesson has yet to be learned that deflation is more dangerous than inflation and, indeed, that a moderate degree of inflation can help lighten the burden of debts grown unsustainable?

The fact that the Bundesbank and the German government are now showing readiness to contemplate a possible increase in prices and wages is, then, to be greeted favourably. It could, in fact, yield beneficial effects for the debtor countries and the entire eurozone, accruing back to Germany itself, and for two reasons. The wage increase would raise disposable income and thus German workers' demand for consumption goods, part of that demand extending to goods produced in other European countries. At the same time, higher prices in Germany could help to smooth out the imbalances in trade that underlie the present tensions between the creditor and debtor countries, which risk splitting Europe asunder.

Only Partial Compensation

Taking all things into consideration, these measures should not in fact be seen as generous gestures by Germany but rather as the recognition of hard realities, a necessary turnabout, departing from behaviour that has contributed, as the exact reverse of the debtor countries' thriftlessness, to creating the eurozone imbalances. In fact, it is precisely by virtue of containing wage and price increases below those of all other European countries that Germany has been able to export and grow at such a steady rate, in the shelter of the single currency.

Thus, Germany has benefited from monetary union. The country's government leaders are reluctant to admit as much in so many words, tending rather to speak of the euro as a heavy burden. But if it were really so heavy, wouldn't Germany be thinking of abandoning the union? Why doesn't Germany withdraw from the euro rather than Greece? Perhaps it's because the single currency suits the countries in surplus at least as much as the countries in deficit.

Apart from the spectre of hyperinflation, it seems likely that these advantages, too, have confirmed Germany in its insistence on the defence of a strong currency. The euro has stopped countries like Italy from making easy gains in competitiveness through devaluation of the nominal exchange rate, but it certainly has not stopped Germany from devaluing its real exchange rate through reduction in relative prices. Indeed, since the introduction of the euro, prices in Germany have increased by little more than 20 per cent, while in Italy they have risen by about 30 per cent. The effect has been a devaluation in Germany's real exchange rate, arriving more stealthily but no less dangerously than the devaluations that the introduction of the euro was meant to prevent. If the roles were to reverse now, and Germany were to take on part of the burden of readjustment, it would simply be a matter of reverting to the rules of the game that, from David Hume on, have always been recognized as fundamental for a fair and balanced international trade.

Nevertheless, we can't help feeling that this may not suffice. Even if Germany finally acquiesces in taking on its part in the adjustment of the real exchange rates, the burden of bearing and addressing European imbalances (which, let us repeat, all the countries have helped create) would continue to fall mainly on the debtors' shoulders. And, as Keynes pointed out way back in the 1940s in the passage quoted and commented on above, the asymmetrical distribution of the burden of adjustment on the debtors' shoulders risks perpetuating the international imbalances to the detriment of all and sundry.

The Dissymmetry Between Creditors and Debtors

The reasons for the dissymmetry are manifold. To begin with, it's a matter of how the imbalance came about: the position of a creditor country is always taken on voluntarily, while that of a debtor country may be dictated by conditions of more or less pressing need. The creditor can always spend more, while the debtor may have to borrow, having no choice but to go on buying whether it has the money or not. A country can be driven into deficit because it can't afford to spend less, but no country is ever driven into surplus since it could always spend more. Once debt arises, and as long as it lasts, it gives rise to an even more evident dissymmetry: the country in deficit bears a burden while the country in surplus enjoys a benefit in the form of the interest paid by the other. And if a country sets out to reduce its debit or credit position, a further dissymmetry appears: to re-balance its external accounts, a country in deficit has to implement restrictive policies, while a country in surplus will have to apply expansionary policies – and the former are far more painful than the latter, as the Greeks know very well, and the Italians, too, are learning. Finally – and again the evidence is before us – the adjustment process is obligatory for the country in deficit, optional for the country in surplus.

If Europe is to get over the impasse, then, the burden of adjustment must be fairly distributed between debtors and creditors, just as the benefits of the imbalance were symmetrically distributed as long as they lasted. One way to do this was devised by Keynes himself with the proposal for the International Clearing Union, unfortunately cast aside at Bretton Woods in favour of a markedly asymmetric system based on the use of the dollar as international currency.

A Clearing House for Europe

The proposal is this: the institution of a European clearing house on the model of the Clearing Union.[9] It may be pictured as an adaptation of the new institution created to address the crisis, the European Stability Mechanism (ESM), with two significant adjustments that would make it swifter and more effective at the same time. To begin with, unlike the ESM, a clearing house would require neither the precautionary allocation of funds nor the granting of huge guarantees by the member countries (with the risk of seeing them thrown out by the respective parliaments or by a sentence from Karlsruhe). Like the Clearing Union, we can picture it as a bank, but with no capital, nor deposits, nor reserves. Quite simply, each country has an account with a clearing house and each account has an initial balance at zero. Each country is granted the possibility to 'go into the red', within set limits, thereby financing a temporary deficit in external accounts. On the other hand, the countries in surplus show a positive balance. In general, each operation entails twofold recording: the same sum is entered as debt for the buyer and credit for the seller. Thanks to this accounting system, the overall clearing house balances are always at zero, which is why no reserves are needed. The second special feature of this bank is that debtors and creditors are treated symmetrically: if the former pay interest on their negative balances, the latter do not gain it, but, on the contrary, pay a commission on their positive balances. This is a measure that may seem exorbitant but, as we pointed out when illustrating how Keynes's Clearing Union worked, it is actually perfectly justified by the fact that the creditors have deposited nothing in the bank and yet benefit from its services, just like debtors: in fact, while the clearing house enables the latter to buy what otherwise they could not have afforded, similarly, and indeed complementarily, it enables the former to sell what otherwise they would have found no market for. Moreover, the symmetrical costs constitute an incentive for creditors and debtors to restore balance in their external accounts. A clearing house thus conceived would open the way to financing internal imbalances in Europe without having to resort to international financial markets, and at the same time ensure that any such imbalances be limited and temporary.

Despite the symmetrical inducements to achieve a balance in external accounts, persistent imbalances could still come about. To address any such eventuality, the Clearing Union made provision for the option, and in some cases the obligation, to adjust the exchange rates between national and international (bancor) currency, devaluing the currency of countries in deficit and revaluing that of the countries in surplus. In order to be able to apply the exchange rate lever for the purpose of adjustment, national currencies would have to be restored, but this would not mean forgoing the euro. The idea is, we believe, well worth considering and need not necessarily entail a flexible exchange rate regime with the consequent fluctuations. After all, not only the Clearing Union but also the Bretton Woods system was designed to function with adjustable rates. In any case, even if the single currency does not allow the adjustment of nominal rates, provision could be made for adjustment of the real rates through differentiated regulation of the price dynamics in the different countries. Of course, this does not mean bringing in an administered price system but simply implementing an appropriate credit and income policy in each country.

The Precedent of the European Payments Union

Fine, of course, but is it feasible? Well, actually it is. In fact, it's already been done – in Europe, just over fifty years ago, in similar circumstances and with extraordinary results.

Having staggered out of the Second World War, Europe had already gone through tens of billions of dollars of Marshall Plan aid, but was still struggling to get back on its feet. Was it to take yet more money? No, all that was needed was a system to enable the countries of Europe to grant each other credit reciprocally in order to start investing once again, and producing, trading and consuming. They arrived at the system in 1950 in the form of a clearing house. In eight years, the European Payments Union literally achieved wonders: the Italian and German economic miracles, trade in Europe increasing twofold, and European trade with the United States threefold; trade was liberalized and a new common, integrated and balanced economic area was created.

Then as now, it was a matter of finding a way out of the paradox of unsatisfied needs that could not be matched with unutilized resources – the paradox of every crisis. Today as then, matching can be eased with the institution of a clearing house: a new European Payments Union could make a real contribution to restoring credibility and vitality to that courageous political and economic project for peace and prosperity which was just beginning to take shape then, and which we now call the European Union, without, however, taking the trouble to design a framework of monetary and financial rules able truly to unite rather than to divide.

Transforming TARGET2 Into a European Clearing Union

Actually, this would not be a matter of reviving something dead and done with. In the eurozone, there already exists a clearing house for the precise purpose of optimizing the management of payments within the area. It's called

TARGET2, and it's the system used by the European Central Bank to manage international payments within the European System of Central Banks.

Increasingly, the debtor countries' balance-of-payments deficits have been financed thanks to this facility since, with the outbreak of the crisis, the customary sources of financing through the inter-bank market and the financial markets began to dry up. Thus, together with the other countries in surplus, in the course of the last five years Germany has accumulated credits for over 800 billion euros within the clearing house while, correspondingly, Portugal, Spain, Greece, Ireland and, in the last year, Italy, too, have together accumulated an equivalent volume of debts.

The European countries hit by the crisis have suffered a flight of capital over the last few years. The outflow of private capital is not to be seen in the balance-of-payments data, having been offset by an inflow of public capital, taking two forms in particular: (1) loans granted within the framework of the programmes for extraordinary funding organized by the International Monetary Fund and the European Union; (2) loans granted to the debtor countries' central banks by the central banks of the creditor countries.

The balance-of-payments imbalances of the eurozone member countries are thus reflected, to some extent at least, in the respective accounts with the TARGET2 system, where the creditor countries of northern Europe had arrived at a positive net cumulated position of 800 billion euros by December 2011, corresponding exactly to the negative net cumulated position of the southern European debtor countries (Figure 3.6).

Thus, through TARGET2, the ECB has made an essential contribution to the financing of the imbalances at a time when private operators were increasingly reluctant to do so. But it hasn't contributed to settling them.

The idea of subjecting these balances to symmetrical charges in accordance with Keynes's Clearing Union model seems, therefore, to be worth considering.[10] The option can,

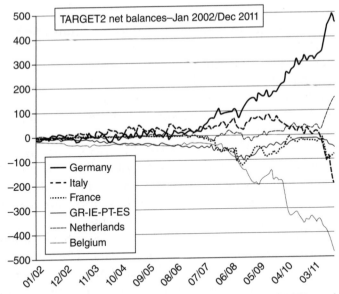

Figure 3.6 A clearing union without clearing (TARGET2 net balances, January 2002–December 2011)
Source: S. Merler and J. Pisani-Ferry, 'Sudden Stops in the Euro Area', Bruegel Policy Contribution, 2012, n. 6

and we believe must, take on the form of a political proposal bringing all the countries to face up to their responsibility in settling the imbalances in so far as they have enjoyed advantages in accumulating them.

This would be a concrete political move in the direction of sanctioning European economic solidarity at the institutional level, unless, of course, the idea is that the creditors are always right and that the appropriate political stance is to side with them. It would serve as a reminder to the creditor countries that they, too, have benefited from the single currency, thanks to the opportunity to export to the countries of southern Europe at a competitive real exchange rate. And it would serve to involve these countries in the adjustment process without having to appeal to their 'kind-heartedness'.

To turn TARGET2 into a clearing house able to reduce imbalances besides financing them, at least four measures would have to be adopted: restriction of credit solely to commercial transactions between European countries; a limit to the possibility of accumulating positive or negative balances, commensurate with each country's volume of foreign trade; a symmetrical rate of interest applying equally to the creditor and debtor countries to induce them to get back into equilibrium; and the possibility of adjusting the real, if not nominal, interest rates, should imbalances prove persistent. The result would be a European Clearing Union in the true sense of the phrase, affording the eurozone countries concrete solidarity such as would in turn restore to the whole of Europe that common sense of purpose that is lacking today.

The ideal – and concrete advantages – of solidarity between debtors and creditors applies not only at the international (global and European) level, but also at the local level. We have already had occasion to mention the projects that are being worked on and, more generally speaking, the need now emerging to reinforce corporate finance at the local level. We must now look into the subject more thoroughly. For some time now, as mentioned, we have been collaborating with several local administrations in Italy and abroad on the design of a local currency and credit circuit involving firms, workers and associations in the third sector. Other projects of the sort have already been launched or are about to be.[11] Here, we wish to illustrate a point that we have in fact been making for a good ten years on the economic, social and political advantageousness of a well-constructed local currency.[12] Outlining what's involved in the construction will lead us to take a fresh and closer look at the basic points underlying our proposals for reform and once again put them to the test.

4

Local Currencies and Local Finance

The doubt to be dispelled from the outset lies in the idea that local currency and credit systems constitute forms of opposition to the official currency and global credit, and thus simply forms of localistic reaction.

This is why the appropriate notion to start from when approaching the whole business of local credit and currency is that of complementarity. The direction indicated by complementarity is not towards closure. To appreciate this point, it will suffice to abandon all blind faith in the principle that a single currency can deal effectively with every task. The fact that it is a commonly accepted principle does not justify sticking to it at all costs. In fact, looking back over history, it is precisely this principle that has for over three centuries implied the dangerous indistinction between national and international currency that we have had frequent occasion to censure.

The present monetary system is based on attributing the role of international currency to a national currency, namely the dollar. Before the dollar, it was the pound sterling, and in fact nothing would change if other national currencies were added to, or replaced, the dollar. While the principle remains debatable, its consequences continue to prove somewhat catastrophic.

What Keynes proposed at Bretton Woods in 1944 was in the first place to bring back the distinction between national and international currency by introducing a pure unit of account at the international level, namely the bancor. In this case, complementarity would be between national and international currencies, the aim being to maintain autonomy in monetary policies at home while pursuing the objective of equilibrium in the balance of trade. For Keynes, then, it was essentially a matter of forging anew the links between domestic economy and foreign trade.

At the same time, a local currency that is not a store of value can be seen as complementary to a reserve currency with a global role to play, such as the euro. Here, the complementarity between local currency and euro serves much the same purpose, linking the local dimension of economic activity in a specific area with openness to international markets.

In this perspective, a local unit of account is all that is needed to launch a scheme for credit clearing between local firms. It will suffice to scale down the system of global and European clearing houses illustrated above to local realities. Instead of countries, we will have firms; instead of imports and exports, clients–supplier relations. The parties involved and the scope of interaction may change, but the advantages offered by the clearing system remain essentially the same. Where the reciprocal interest lies in reciprocal and balanced trade in goods and services, clearing ensures that lack of money need never stand in the way of activities that appear creditworthy. At the same time, clearing does away with the equal and opposite risk of an excess of fiduciary money leading to inflation since the money created in anticipation is symmetrically destroyed when the debtors pay their debts and the creditors spend their credits.[1]

For the clearing to work at the local level, the firms involved must have part of their clients and part of their suppliers operating within the area. And it is precisely the degree of participation by each firm in the local economy, as well of course as its creditworthiness, that determines the optimal degree of its participation in the clearing system, or in other words the limit or quota for positive and negative balances alike. In the logic of a clearing system, firm A will accept to be paid in the local unit of account by firm B, just as it knows it will be able to spend with another firm, N, belonging to the circuit.

Thus, the spending capacity counts as much as the selling capacity in determining the degree of a firm's participation in the circuit. The first criterion for limitation which we have already seen at work in the case of the Clearing Union plan, i.e., the setting of symmetric limits (or quotas) on debt and credit balances, is also of the utmost relevance to a local system. In this case, too, the only position truly desirable in economic terms is that of a tendentiously balanced budget. Indeed, it is even more so if, also benefiting from the past experience of WIR and the more recent example of Sardex, the firms holding assets can never, in any case, request and obtain conversion of their local currency balances into euros.

While free to exit from the circuit when they choose, on exiting, firms lose all rights over their positive balances within the circuit. In a 'hermetic' clearing system, the only sensible criterion for the use of credit balances lies, therefore, in spending them. In so far as the firms comply scrupulously and intelligently, the second criterion set by Keynes, i.e., application of a negative interest rate on positive balances, could even prove economically unnecessary, or at least secondary.

Indeed, unlike the scheme Keynes devised for international trade, designed essentially to facilitate return to equilibrium in the balance of trade, a local clearing system can be explicitly tied to local currency circulation and payment of wages. While a firm selling locally may not necessarily have its suppliers in the same area, its spending on wages is always local. Here, in fact, we have a further possibility, which can transform a local clearing circuit into an effective monetary circuit: if the appropriate agreements can be reached between firms and workers, for example through bargaining at the regional or firm level, using the local

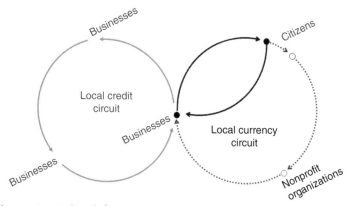

Figure 4.1 A local finance system

currency for wages opens the way to local monetary circulation, supporting local demand and thus production (Figure 4.1).

With a monetary circuit in operation alongside the credit circuit, the economic significance of the local currency is enhanced. Wages paid in the local currency translate entirely into local demand for local commodities, affording support for the clearing system among firms. Bearing in mind the fact that within a clearing system spending and selling capacity are equally important, if the assets accumulated by firms are no longer necessarily to be spent on the goods/services of other firms but can be used for the workers' wages, then the quota of each firm can rise significantly.

Moreover, if a firm also uses its credit to pay its workers, it can accept to be paid more extensively through the clearing system and so enjoy greater scope in selling its goods to other firms, while the purchasing power in the hands of workers will be an inducement for firms producing or selling consumption goods to enter into the circuit. They will then be able to receive credit from the workers and spend it on the goods/services of their suppliers within the clearing circuit.

Thus, increasing together with the number of firms belonging to the circuit will be the quota of transactions which each of them will be able to pay in the local currency. The twofold effect thereby produced is an increase in the proportion of local trade mediated through the local currency and in the range of goods and services available within the circuit. The two advantages enter into reciprocal reinforcement, providing support for the circuit to grow.

Including workers in the circuit also opens up a further possibility. A rate of negative interest (or decumulation) could be applied to the balances of individuals with the effect of accelerating monetary circulation yet further, preventing stagnation of the local currency on individuals' current accounts and helping it find its way back to the firms' accounts.

On top of this purely functional advantage, there could also be a further possibility for development of the system, which would enhance its social significance. If it were applied to the balances of the individual participants, the decumulation could amount to something more than mere destruction of purchasing power, implying thorough transformation. In fact, the decumulation could take the form of transference of part of a participant's current-account balance (for example, 0.5 per cent per month) to another account in the name of the same participant but serving a different end. While remaining in the possession of the same individual, the amount transferred could no longer be used to buy goods or services, but should be given to a non-profit organization chosen by the individual. Decumulation would thus give rise to a flow of local purchasing power to operators in the local third sector. What individuals do not spend on goods for private use can thus be transferred to non-profit organizations for the supply of common goods and services of social utility. Given that the money at their disposal will be spent entirely in the directions pursued by non-profit organizations, the latter could function as 'spenders of last resort' in the system, or in other words as final guarantors for the non-stagnation of the local currency or, to put it in positive terms, as accelerators of the local currency's velocity of circulation.

A further boost to the growth of the clearing circuit and the local currency's velocity of circulation could be offered by the public administration if it decided to accept, at least partially, the local currency to pay for services and eventually certain local taxes, and put it back into circulation by paying suppliers and part of employees' wages with it.

One last point: credit clearing could work in relations not only between firms but also between individuals on the model of the 'time banks', but with the advantage of also being able to use local currency to pay firms without the obligation to tie the transfer of credit between people to the exchange of favours on the basis of hours worked by each.

The Individual Advantages of the Local Credit and Currency Circuits

We have seen how a credit clearing scheme can serve as a basis upon which to build a local currency system able both to support local trade and to link up market economy with social economy. It is now time to look more closely at the advantages such a scheme can hold both for the community as a whole and for the individual categories of participants.

Let us start with the advantages for firms. As we have seen, the most immediate and devastating effect of the liquidity crisis on firms, and in particular on the small and medium-sized firms, is the indiscriminate clampdown on credit. By sharing in a local clearing circuit, the local system of firms is able to make up for the lack of credit for trade carried out amongst them at the local level. The more intensive the interaction between the firms proves, the greater will be the liquidity requirements that the clearing house will be able to satisfy. It is the firms themselves as a whole that serve as a bank for the firms, reciprocally providing credit in the form of deferred payment, not on bilateral terms, but on a multilateral basis. This represents no small advantage, and so it is effectively perceived to judge by the ongoing multiplication of multilateral corporate barter schemes.[2]

To begin with, belonging to the local credit clearing circuit enables the firm to finance its circulating capital without any need to resort to the traditional banking system. It needs no great stretch of the imagination to appreciate the advantage of credit mutualized with the clearing system: the firms have access to liquidity created and destroyed through the rhythm of their trade and need not acquire money from banks that in turn acquire it on the market. This means lower costs for financing. In other words, borrowing through the clearing house costs less than getting credit from a bank. In fact, the bank also has to charge its debtors for the cost of the money it has to borrow on the market. By contrast, the clearing house bears no cost in obtaining money to lend to a purchaser since it generates local currency itself whenever it registers credit in favour of a seller. Moreover, as we have seen, the credit in local currency receives no interest, and can even be subjected to negative interest, in which case creditors together with debtors share in covering the costs of running the clearing house. We might say that, much like the banks, the clearing house also covers its running costs by virtue of the spread between the rates of interest applied to its credit and the rates applied to its liabilities except that, in the case of the clearing house, the former are zero, if not actually negative.

To make the point even clearer, let us compare the clearing house with an ordinary bank. Like any enterprise, both have to cover their costs with their gains. For both, these costs include all the expenses that have to be borne in accurate assessment of the debtors' creditworthiness and adequate monitoring (say, for example, amounting to 3% of the sum of credit supplied). Added to these, for the bank, are the costs of acquiring the money, i.e. of the interest rate it has to pay, on average, to its creditors (say, 4%). The bank has to charge its debtors a rate of interest sufficient to cover both its running costs and the costs entailed in acquiring the money (in our example, 3% + 4% = 7%). By contrast, acquisition costs for the clearing house are zero inasmuch as it does not remunerate credits in the local currency, and actually negative if it applies a decumulation rate to the credits. Thus, the clearing house is able to charge its debtors a rate of interest that is in all cases equal to the algebraic sum of running costs and acquisition costs, with the latter being, however, zero or negative. For example, taking the case of a decumulation rate on credit amounting to 1.5%, the debtors will also have to pay a rate of 1.5% on their debts (= 3% − 1.5%).

Besides the financial saving, belonging to a multilateral clearing circuit implies in itself a comparative advantage resulting from the mere presence of the firm in the circuit. Inasmuch as it is ready to accept payment in the local currency, a firm participating in it becomes more interesting for its clients than a firm outside the circuit, since they will be able to rely on a less costly means of payment. The availability of an alternative and less costly channel for payment thus reinforces relations between local firms while also forming the basis for progressive extension of the circuit. Both the clients and the suppliers of a member firm will find it in their interest to join the circuit and accept payment in the local currency precisely to the extent that they can anticipate in turn having clients and suppliers interested in engaging in trade with the clearing system. The overall effect is a standardized sign of distinction marking out the firms participating: all other conditions being equal, any firm in the system will favour relations with other such firms rather than firms outside the circuit, attracted by the reduced costs (compared with cash payment) and greater reciprocal trust (compared to deferred payment), all the firms having an interest in transparent behaviour as an essential condition to remain in the circuit and continue enjoying its benefits.

Thirdly, an advantage for all participants, regardless of their position, is an increase in their turnover, for the firms belonging to the clearing circuit are in a better position to sell their products and services, being able at the same time to access a wider pool of demand. Thanks to the system, firms can acquire goods and services that they would not otherwise have been able to afford and, complementarily, they can sell products that would otherwise have been collecting dust in the warehouse. Thus, the macroeconomic effect is support for income generated by the higher velocity of circulation of money. Naturally, this macroeconomic effect is further enhanced if part of the wages is paid in local currency. By the very fact that it is thus denominated and cannot be spent outside the circuit, the percentage of total wages paid in the local currency can find no employment other than being rapidly and entirely transformed into local demand for local products.

The advantage that firms enjoy by paying part of their wages in local currency is fairly evident, in terms both of costs, thanks to lighter financial expenses, and of revenues, this part of the wages being entirely channelled into local demand for local firms as a whole. Not quite so evident is the advantage for the workers, which has to be structured through bargaining at the firm or regional level.

At the outset, in so far as it affords a saving in firms' financial expenses, transition to the local currency may immediately entail transference of part of this saving to the workers in the form of wage benefits. It would thus be a way of distributing between firms and workers the advantage deriving from lower financial costs. In macroeconomic terms, it can be described as a redistribution of total income, from financial rents to profits and wages.

But in addition the advantages over the medium period, and their distribution, can be approached in the same spirit of a local policy of income redistribution in favour of workers and entrepreneurs. The support for local production constituted by local demand in local currency implies in turn support for local employment and a disincentive to de-localize. On the basis of 'well-tempered' and well-concerted agreements, provision could then be made for wage increases in the medium period, while at the same time the firms take on the commitment of investing more in the local area. The spirit is that of a local income policy in the form of explicit collaboration between firms and workers within the local area with a view to development of the area and its competitive potential. Today, as never before, the possibility of a pact between producers to put up a common defence against the depressive effects of financial rent merits most serious consideration.

Introducing a local currency as an instrument for industrial relations remains a very delicate matter, immediately raising a question that must absolutely be reckoned with, namely on what conditions can payment of part of total wages prove economically, socially and juridically acceptable? Well before the circuit is launched, firms and unions should examine the issues involved in depth and without preconceptions.

We may, however, anticipate a few points. There are three major aspects to consider when addressing the question. To begin with, the local currency should not entail a 'saving' for the firm in terms of social security taxes: when wages are paid in the local currency, these taxes must be calculated on the corresponding amount in euro. Secondly, the net effect on the overall wage must prove comparatively positive; in other words, the cumulative effect of payment in euros and in local currency must add up, over the medium period, to an increase in overall purchasing power for the workers. Effectively, this is the advantage that can induce the workers to accept payment in the local currency while at the same time accepting decumulation on their balance. At the same time, the increase in overall payments to workers should not represent too heavy a burden for firms, since all that they agree to advance to the workers in the local currency rapidly translates into increased turnover for the firms in the circuit as a whole. Thirdly, payment in the local currency must apply to all the parties involved in the life of the firm, including management and owners. If and to the extent that transition is accomplished adequately and in general agreement, the economic significance of the entire circuit is greatly enhanced.

And enhancement is all the fuller if decumulation takes the form of transformation of individual purchasing power into an equally individual 'donation duty', as described above. For that part of their balance that is subject to the negative interest rate, the individuals belonging to the circuit become direct financial backers of the third sector. The advantage that non-profit organizations derive from belonging to a local credit and currency scheme is so evident that it can be counterbalanced by a requirement for maximum transparency in reporting the criteria for spending the financing thus received.

The Systemic Advantages of Local Credit and Currency Circuits

A complementary local currency and credit system entails ample participation and, while involvement in terms of ideals is obviously desirable, each participant must be able to appreciate a good economic basis for joining in the form of support for their budgets. This is an essential condition if the local credit system is to evolve from the free enterprise of its participants, with no sense of obligation. Once launched, the system will then generate further advantages that can corroborate the initial decision and attract still greater participation, enhancing the economic virtuousness of the circuit. It is in fact essential to achieve a 'critical mass' in terms both of the number of participants and the range of goods and services offered for the credit and monetary mechanisms to exert positive effects not only for individual participants but also for the system as a whole.

What, then, are these systemic advantages? To begin with, there is a territorial integration effect. Within one area, which is also a political and economic area, citizens, firms and associations of the third sector can form and reinforce reciprocal relations of collaboration. Restoring finance to the local level, far from implying a closed community, opens the way for the reorganization of the components of local social and economic life, and indeed provides prospects for communities in the area to play a more substantial role in global competition.

At the same time, an economy does not live solely on the purely economic relations it engenders, but also on the air breathed within it. An economic context necessarily forms part of a broader system of relations that are not readily susceptible to monetization, but which ultimately affect the cost structure, too. The economists refer to all this as 'externalities'. Now, a well-constructed local currency helps to hold local society together, supporting the local economy in such a way that it does not react to crisis by cutting spending but helps to hold close the skills that have been developed in the area over decades, making resort to de-localization less attractive. Shrewdly managed, all these effects are in fact susceptible to monetization in that they help maintain a healthy level of productivity in the area.

Let us try a different angle. 'Global finance' has called for and continues to depend on the flexibility and de-localization of human resources, simply because the only measure of 'performance' that matters to it is the profitability of the financial capital channelled into portfolio investments and forever on the point of changing direction. By contrast, re-localizing finance inverts the hierarchic relationship between real economy and finance. By virtue of it, the criteria for evaluation of performance can and indeed must be less abstract than the standards implied by financial rent-seeking. The formula runs thus: while the principle of global liquid finance sees labour solely as a resource to exploit, it is skills that come into sight with the re-localization of finance, in so far as it also brings into play the network of relations existing where the work is being performed. Where finance begins to take root once again in the local economy, the economy can become manifest in its structure as a system of economic and social relations. In the last few years, there has been much talk of the local territory as a resource and 'identity-making' element, in contrast with the considerations advanced on globalization. Perhaps things are rather simpler than they appear through such contrasting positions: perhaps, as the economist Alfred Marshall observed with respect to industrial districts, an economic area is essentially 'in the air' breathed together. One aspect of enhancing free-market relations on the basis of a market tool like the complementary currency is the possibility to go on breathing the same air precisely because the life-breath of credit is generated reciprocally. A local credit clearing scheme constitutes rationalization, generalization and implementation of the principle of giving room for trade to breathe.

To put it yet another way: in practice, a local clearing house of the type described here is a local public bank dedicated to financing the system of small and medium-sized firms which, in Italy as in France and elsewhere, constitutes the soil of the economy. It's a public bank not because it uses public capital, retaining or even, with a view to patronage, dangerously slackening the management criteria of a private commercial bank. It's a public bank because the rationale behind the service it offers is public. The bank is public, and the credit the participants mutually concede is cooperative. For once, we have an innovation that does not aim to destroy public space in the name of the distributive efficiency attributed, with blind faith, to financial mechanisms. A public bank thus conceived is a pure financial intermediary: it sells and buys nothing, but holds together in potentially virtuous relations debtors and creditors with a view to a balanced reduction of the pressure coming ceaselessly from the market financial system. For these reasons, too, the integration favoured by the complementary currency means neither that local communities close in on themselves, nor that they join forces 'against': primarily, it offers scope for local needs and initiatives to take on a new configuration.

Again with regard to the public and political function of the local complementary currency, there is yet another consideration to be made. A credit clearing system based on a complementary currency could favour effective interaction between an 'exchange economy' and a 'gift economy' or, better still, between an exchange economy in the strict sense and in the broad sense. We say interaction, and not juxtaposition or hierarchization or marginalization. The flow of purchasing power to the third sector thanks to decumulation endows the third sector with the power to address firms as equals in every sense, equally integrated in the economy. Representing 'social demand', the third sector enters into relations with firms, calling on them to adjust their supply to its needs. And above all, the relationship between firms and the third sector is freed from any ambiguity insomuch as financing of the third sector is realized through the individual choices of citizens rather than donations by firms. This means an end to the ambiguity that has all too long marked those practices that go under the name of 'corporate social responsibility'. In so far as they cease to be direct financial supporters of the third sector, the firms will return to what is supposed to be their primary task: responding efficiently to demand for goods and services.

Local integration supported by the complementary local currency entails in itself an increase in the volume of trade within the community on the part of those belonging to the monetary and credit circuit. Given that this is achieved essentially through the increased velocity of circulation of the local monetary instruments, no injections of liquidity will be needed to feed the increase. The anti-depressive effect is clear: the trade itself generates money and ceases to depend on the decisions to hoard money that characterize liquidity crises (liquidity trap and credit crunch). For the same reason that lies behind its anti-depressive effect, a currency and credit circuit based on the principle of clearing engenders no risk of inflation. The macroeconomic effect of support for demand relies neither on an increase in the quantity of money nor on an increase in local public spending, but derives entirely from the increase in trade itself and in the velocity of currency circulation.

Indeed, from the point of view of the national budget, the introduction of a clearing system could help boost internal revenue in so far as it effectively raises the volume of trade. In fact, the idea is that payments in local currency are neutral from the point of view of the revenue authorities, i.e., all normal taxes on payments in the official currency apply to them. The increase in internal revenue could be further boosted by the elimination of cash-in-hand payments: in fact, the local currency is electronic, and all transactions in it are perfectly traceable.

In terms of local public spending, too, the effect is not to be seen in increase but rather containment, or, symmetrically, an increase in social policies with no change in public spending. The additional financing channelled into the third sector through monetary decumulation serves to support the local welfare system with no increase in local borrowing or taxation. Obviously, the third sector cannot substitute public welfare entirely, but, based on the principle of subsidiarity combined with a direct, decentralized form of financing, complementarity in the field of social policies, too, can prove as practicable as it is desirable.

Last but by no means least, taking into particular consideration the situation in Italy and the concern recently shown over the public administrations' dilatoriness in payment, a public administration belonging to a local clearing system could cease to weigh on the financial structure of firms kept waiting all too long for payment. That clearing between public administration debt and credit vis-à-vis firms variously invoked, all sorts of expedients more or less compatible with the legal and fiscal system being suggested, would become a perfectly routine and verifiable operation within a local clearing circuit.

The other significant social effect is, as we have seen, the contribution offered by the complementary currency circuit to reorganizing wage bargaining at the local level. A system for paying wages that lightens the burden for firms while proving more attractive to workers, as well as according with labour law protecting the dignity of labour, could have the effect of making flexibility and de-localization less obvious options, even following pure market-based calculations. Indeed, flexibility and de-localization may appear to be the only options as long as global market finance is seen to have no alternatives. With the re-localization of finance, there is also the opportunity to re-localize labour markets with consequently closer focus on the skills that every local economy has accumulated over time, and which can become a far more interesting competitive factor than simple advantage in terms of wages.

Here we come once again to an aspect that merits closer examination at this point. We might say that a well-constructed local currency – a currency that is not a mere replica of the official currency on a smaller scale – is essentially cooperative.

Local Currency as a Tool for Cooperation

In the opening pages of this book, we identified a strong factor behind the persistence of the market finance paradigm in the belief that there is no alternative. We also suggested that perception of the possibility of an alternative could open up on escaping from the vice-like hold of the state–market antithesis because the finance of global financial markets requires and rests upon a strange and unconfessed alliance between the two – strange, unconfessed, and, moreover, asymmetric.

Before the crisis, the idea had emerged from all the talk about 'democratization of finance' that financial globalization, with the guiding principle of liquidity, could open the way to 'cooperation' in an ambiguous form of a game in which everyone wins and no one loses. The creditors run no risks, and the debtors don't actually pay. But precisely this promise of a land flowing with milk and honey should have put us on our guard. What characterizes a spirit of cooperation is not the idea that everyone always wins but, rather, the fact that, win or lose, the boons and burdens are borne together and proportionately. Any other form of 'cooperation' is simply perverse.

In fact, the sharing not only of advantages but also of risks is an inherently characteristic feature of finance based on the clearing principle. We've said it before, and it certainly bears repeating: the relationship between debtor and creditor is in itself cooperative; were it not so, it would cease to exist as a relationship. Precisely because it is based on the pseudo-principle of liquidity, the financial innovation of the last few decades has aimed systematically at eliminating, or at least giving the impression of having eliminated, the risk structurally associated with the debtor–creditor relationship.

The liquidity dogma and the clearing principle have no points in common, as we have seen from the outset. Now, however, we have some further elements to illustrate and bring more light to bear on the benefits of a new form of finance, which is not a market finance, but, for this very reason, is a finance for the market, as can be achieved with the implementation of a local currency and credit circuits.

In a clearing system, by the very fact that it derives from the decision to await payment, credit is structurally cooperative. On the strength of this decision, the creditor is able to sell goods which otherwise he would have risked not selling, and the debtor can purchase goods which otherwise he could not have afforded, without having to obtain liquidity on payment. While the debtor is committed to paying through selling goods that he will be able to produce by having obtained supplies on credit, the creditor in turn takes on a commitment, namely to spend his credit purchasing goods and services.

Thanks to the multilateral organization of the system, the cooperative element inherent in every single debtor–creditor relationship takes on even greater solidity. While individual responsibilities and abilities remain essential, it is the creditors as a whole who, spending their credit, enable debtors to pay; just as it is the debtors as a whole who, paying their debts, allow creditors to have something to buy. In a nutshell, the cooperative aspect of clearing lies in the fact that the economic behaviour of the individuals is not only compatible with pursuit of a common advantage, but actually drives structurally in that direction.

Credit is cooperative by virtue of the fact that the clearing system brings about the convergence towards balance between all the participants' balances. Similarly, thanks to the decumulation tool, that is, the transformation of individuals' purchasing powers into a flow of financing towards the third sector, the monetary circulation generates cooperation between exchange economy and gift economy, or in other words between exchange economy in the strict sense and exchange economy in the broad sense. The economic circuit of production and trade, on the one hand, and the social circuit of (re)distribution on the other not only come into contact but enter into reciprocal reinforcement. The economic function of decumulation – speeding up circulation to the extent of stemming any tendency to hoard – results in a flow of funds and assets that are not strictly speaking economic, but which reinforce the social fabric where production is performed while at the same time entailing economic activities for their implementation. Not only are the funds that arrive in the third sector not removed from circulation, but they actually increase the velocity of trade.

Finally, if local currency gives rise to new forms of local wage bargaining, then industrial relations themselves can take on a more distinctly cooperative nature. Such cooperation could be seen as an alliance of labour (in all its forms, including both wage labour and entrepreneurial labour) against the demands and undue pressures of financial rent-seeking. This is clearly a delicate matter, but it has the virtue of bringing together two needs that have even come to seem incompatible in recent years: the need to safeguard labour and the need to safeguard free economic activity. Indeed, a complementary local currency can cover the interests of labour and economic liberalism alike. So much can be demonstrated. However, before any demonstration, there is a point to be made which may appear intuitive: globalized market finance tends to squeeze out the local labour market, leaving no room for any form of bargaining with a view to some sort of social contract between the productive forces. Financial globalization has reduced labour to a mere cost to be minimized. A local currency and finance could offer the market the tools and conditions for a new configuration of labour–money exchange to take into account the fact that in the end, returning to a point we made above and taking the cue from Polanyi, neither labour nor money is a commodity. And whether or not there is a social sense to money depends on its capacity to reward labour as fully as possible.

Local money and credit constitute a major means for redefinition at the local level of the social contract both between the components of the productive system and between the exchange economy and that gift economy that silently supports every exchange economy which recognizes its origins in a community.[3] A currency, devoid of the store of value function, circulates – accumulation being pointless – and is lent in ways and at times quite different from those dictated by financial capitalism. A currency, as Keynes observed, is truly such when it 'flows from one hand to another, is received and is dispensed, and disappears when its work is done from the sum of a nation's wealth'.[4] A currency which is not a store of value but a pure unit of account, as in a clearing system, continuously reminds all its users that money and wealth are not the same thing, and that the only proper use for money is to spend it, i.e., to get rid of it. The collective, cooperative liberation of money lies precisely in its circulation and its function in releasing from debt.

Feasibility and Prospects for Development of Local Currency and Credit Systems

Even in the earliest texts where Keynes began to expound his project for reform of the international monetary system, he was already anticipating the objections that he knew would be coming, more or less in good faith, from all sides: the project is very interesting, but hardly feasible; actually, impossible – in a word, 'utopian'. The good thing about this notion of utopia is that it keeps everyone happy, 'dreamers' and 'realists' alike. The dreamers can go on dreaming, imagining a 'better world', while the realists can justify the sombre faces they show with the demands of realpolitik.

Keynes is not deterred. His project is no utopia – or something for which there is no place – but 'eutopia', a good place to be able to inhabit. Although the pronunciation of the two words is the same, they are distinguished by something very different which we might, perhaps, call the 'spirit of political innovation'.

Over the last thirty years, financial innovation has taken on the form of a project to dismantle every political component of economic life in the name of a plan to reconstitute society starting from 'economic logic', i.e., the logic that lies behind the functioning of the 'market'.

Some of us have attempted to remind the exponents of neoliberalism that the market is a social and political construction, but to little effect. So why the stony ground? Perhaps it's because neoliberalism has become a project, in its way political, to dismantle 'politics' – politics not so much in the sense of bureaucratic management of the *res publica* as, rather, in its manifestation in a common place and as a common measure for the life of each and everyone – common, and not subject to private appropriation.

This is why political innovation has taken the form of financial innovation in the doctrine and practice of neoliberalism. The basic idea was and remains very simple: if, thanks to liquidity, the financial markets can spread so far and wide as to function without any interruption, they will guarantee everyone, even though possibly not all at the same time, access to all resources. This, and this alone, was the ultimate justification for the democratization of finance. Basically, it was a matter of agreeing to a modest Faustian bargain: we rid the financial market of every restraint to its expansion and it will benefit us with resources for all, and no one will have to worry about anyone – planned individualism and heterogeneity of ends. Hurrah for Mandeville and down with all the rest.

In the midst of a financial crisis which is also a crisis resulting from an unrealistic way of representing the economy, how are we to regain a sense of reality in economics and politics?

Discussing his plan, Keynes says that 'It is open to objection that it is complicated and novel and perhaps Utopian in the sense, not that it is impracticable, but that it assumes a higher degree of understanding, of the spirit of bold innovation, and of international cooperation and trust than it is safe or reasonable to assume.'[5] With the reference to 'understanding', Keynes is challenging those economists who, having realized what is in fact at stake, may be interested in working on the concrete possibilities opening up that have an alternative principle for organizing finance. It is something we have been working on for some time, and we are not alone in this. Indeed, the ranks are swelling, for it is becoming increasingly clear to a growing number of economists that many elements in economic theory, beginning with the theory of comparative advantages, are far more compatible with a market finance based on clearing than with a market finance based on liquidity.

It is not, however, only at the level of theory that things are moving. Increasingly evident and widespread is a spontaneous trend among economic operators to implement finance schemes alternative to market finance. We have presented some of the evidence here. Thus, we have all the elements to conclude a 'new alliance' between economic operators, politicians and scientists, no longer based on ideological assumptions, and above all freed from that aggravating scientism consisting in the conviction that the economy is a mechanism to study and implement, and not a field to be cultivated. Let us leave to the technocrats the task which only they seem to enjoy of forcing realities to fit with doctrinaire schemes originating from they no longer know where, and let us try working and thinking afresh.

So where does politics come in? Actually, if one thinks about it, the very existence of an economy is in itself political. The spirit of innovation and cooperation that Keynes invoked can in fact emerge from recognition of the fundamentally political nature of every economic institution. Acknowledgement of the failure of attempts to deny this fact of life – a failure epitomized by this crisis, for those who have eyes to see – should encourage the advocates of modernization through political programmes to get to work, and to realize that the only form of political prudence open to us lies in the courage and intelligence to leave the obsolete well behind us.

The Political Stakes

Let us now see how the picture that emerged from discussion of reform at the international level might turn out at the local level – with the necessary adjustments, of course, but also maintaining all the basic analogies.

The first analogy to maintain lies in the impossibility of imposing a credit clearing system – an impossibility that is not only legal and institutional, but also political. Whether at the international or the local level, only with the free accord of all the parties qualified to join can a cooperative credit system function, given that at both levels a good range of participants constitutes a basic structural feature. The complementary currency is private as far as acceptance is concerned, but public in its effects in maintaining and enhancing cohesion amongst those using it.

The need then is to arrive at a constituent agreement ratifying a convergence of objectives determined through independent evaluation of the individual advantages that participation entails. But the path to take to arrive at such an agreement is far from evident, and attention must turn to an appropriate body – public, private or mixed, it matters little – to take on the task of proposing, illustrating and supporting the project. At the outset, the role of this body is probably no less essential than the readiness of the individual participants to commit themselves to a constituent agreement.

This essential combination of a certain spontaneity on the part of the participants and a capacity for guidance on the part of the promoter is to find correspondence in the form taken by the governance of the circuit. In view, precisely, of what this involves, the promoter cannot take command as controller of the circuit. This implies, from the very outset, not only developing real dialogue, but also organizing a form of association compatible with effective participation in management by all the components.

For the credit clearing scheme as such, the legal status of consortium could suffice since that which is to be organized and managed in multilateral terms is known in legal language as the 'assignment of receivables', and only firms are involved. As for the clearing house operations, the main activities are bookkeeping and the evaluation of creditworthiness, the major difficulty lying in handling any cases of unpaid loans arising, for example, from the bankruptcies of individual participants and management of relations with creditors outside the system if the bankrupt holds assets. It could even be an additional service supplied by a cooperative bank to its clients.

On the other hand, if credit and debit clearing is explicitly tied in with a complementary currency circuit involving the participation of workers and, more generally, of citizens, then the harmonization of the diverse positions and points of view must find due representation from the outset.

The introduction of a local currency calls for intensive consultation in the first place, and subsequently adequate governance over its management, since the operational decisions become increasingly complex and must take into account the points of view of all the participants as well as the exigencies involved in the smooth running of the circuit as a whole.

To take but one example, the Italian Fondazione di Partecipazione seems particularly suited to this end. The Fondazione di Partecipazione combines the firm's operational capacities with the possibility of representing all the parties involved in the circuit within an associative environment. It is in fact an institute created with the precise purpose of offering a meeting point between exchange economy and third sector, and the results have so far proved decidedly satisfactory.

A governance structure as cooperative in its functioning as the relations it has to govern should represent and link up internally all the interests that a local currency and credit circuit must be able to mobilize to have a fair chance of success. It would also be the ideal place to continue experimentation in the new form of collaboration between public and private interests which the local currency depends on and at the same time fosters.

Moreover, the need for territorial and local rootedness does not imply a closed system but can, in fact, prompt experimentation in forms of collaborative federalism. With the prospect of a multiplicity of local circuits – still a matter of 'things to come', but no less realistic for that reason – we can start thinking about their interrelations, which could indeed take the form of a federation. This federation would offer scope for interchange amongst circuits, not only reproducing the structure of relations between the firms and between areas but also modifying them accordingly.

What applies for countries and the international community also applies at the local level: the currency is an element of primary importance in the development of free, cohesive communities. Indeed, the better they cohere, the freer they will be, above all in view of the fact that the currency to be introduced locally would function in a manner entirely in keeping with this end.

In short, to return to Keynes's observations, it is quite likely that the virtues of understanding, of bold innovation, of cooperation and trust needed to introduce a local currency may subsequently be enhanced through its functioning.

The political component belongs to the economy as an intrinsic feature of its functioning as an economy. The economy is political if it is a true economy, and it's a true economy if it rests on the foundation of a currency able to keep freedom of economic action and social cohesion together.

Too Good to be True?

The local complementary currency is in every sense a currency because it is a means of linkage – between the local dimension and the international vocation of a territory, between the demands that competitiveness implies for a firm and the dignity of labour, between the economic dimension and the social dimension.

By linkage, we mean holding together different interests within a unit that does not cancel out the differences but brings them into play to their reciprocal advantage. Thus, the need is not for forced 'convergence', nor indeed for standardization, but, more simply, for cooperation.

Cooperation is to the economy what democracy is to politics. It is not based solely on recognizing equality in freedom, but it also requires full recognition of an individual's competences. As Charles Péguy would have said, the only authority that does not imply hierarchies is the authority of competence. In a cooperative context, each does what he or she must do according to their competences by virtue of the fact that everyone else does likewise and, by the same token, they benefit from their activity only by leaving others the opportunity to benefit from theirs.

A local currency – and ultimately any true currency – is a cooperative instrument that goes through everyone's hands, used to trade not only in things but also in words. It is the currency of people who work together and for one another. What our experience is showing us ever more clearly is that, as is emerging from the more serious and innovative projects, a local currency is a currency that gets people talking to each other.

Here, in a few words, we have a fundamental difference between the finance we know and the finance we could have: in the case of a finance for the market, the currency is a means of dialogue, and the exchange it allows is not only at the level of commodities but also at the political level, reciprocally freeing up new areas. We are accustomed to a capitalistic currency that silences and propagates incommunicability – from the commonality, obsessed with finance, stressed and increasingly enraged, to the governing classes, who have increasing difficulty in finding words to talk to one another and to the citizens they are supposed to represent and govern. Real dialogue has been falling out of common practice, but it is time to restore it. When the habitual exercise of dialogue falls short, the two widespread consequences are short-sightedness and deafness.

There is a growing incapacity to take the long-term view of things. This is a flaw inherent in market finance, for which only the very short term exists, while for the long period the glib observation has to suffice that sooner or later equilibrium arrives and growth picks up.

Deafness is at the same time both cause and effect of the incapacity to talk to one another. In a period of crisis, as we are now experiencing, the great risk is to harp on about points of contrast at the expense of rare opportunities for dialogue, above all in the minefield of industrial relations. At the international level, too, there is a growing temptation for countries under economic pressure to ease off with beggar-thy-neighbour strategies.

The alleged rationalism of the neoliberal doctrine on the financial markets has tried to pass off the idea that market efficiency calls for calculation, not dialogue. In this respect, the neoliberal rationale lies in a technocratic logic. And yet this economicist rationalism may prove far from politically and economically reasonable. Chesterton memorably defined a madman as someone who has lost everything but his reason.

So perhaps the time has come to start being less rationalistic and more reasonable. We must learn to recognize the vast distance separating rationality from reasonableness. Leibniz was well aware of it, as indeed was Pascal, observing that the heart has its reasons which reason knows nothing of. And Keynes took it into account when he pointed out the need for animal spirits to support and supplement calculation when the possibilities of calculation have been exhausted.[6]

In economics, 'animal spirits' is an expression referring to the courage, indeed that particularly patient form of courage, that we call by the rather old-fashioned name of longanimity: the ability to hold out even when it isn't quite clear why you should. When, for example, you go on making sacrifices although the rewards never seem to materialize.

Longanimity is the cardinal virtue of the entrepreneur and, in general, it is the only virtue that can help us over short-sightedness and deafness in economic matters. It is the true antidote to that 'short-termism' that characterizes capitalism – the inability to think, and by now perhaps even to calculate, over the long term.

The true economy is that of the worker and entrepreneur, who are well aware that you pay first to make gains afterwards, that you bear the costs first and then receive the proceeds: first you sow, then you reap; first you work, then you eat. And precisely for this reason, one is always, structurally, a debtor. For the rentier, it's the other way round, but then of course his is a pseudo-economy.

Today, sacrifices are being asked of us. What we need to know is: in the name of what? If it's in the name of the conservative programme of return to capitalism, it's hard to see any point in making sacrifices. But if it's in the name of a project to build an economy where the difference is clear between what there is a market for and what there must be no market for, then it's hard to see why we shouldn't get on with it. The question becomes, when do we begin?

It takes more courage to talk to others than it does to stand against them. Cooperation enables mutual encouragement, and in times of crisis it is the only source of strength for facing together the risk that the rentier flees, leaving others to bear the burden. And it is only with this strength that we can really get down to work.

Notes

Introduction

1 For a critique of the neoliberal concept of 'virtual senate', cf. N. Chomsky, *Hopes and Prospects*, Chicago: Haymarket Books, 2010, pp. 97–9.
2 *The Financial Crisis and the Role of Federal Regulators*, 23 October 2008, House of Representatives, Committee on Oversight and Government Reform, Stenographic Minutes, Washington, DC, Office of the Clerk, Office of Official Reporters, ll. 831–66.
3 J. N. Baghwati, 'The Capital Myth: The Difference between Trade in Widgets and Dollars', *Foreign Affairs*, May–June 2008.
4 J. M. Keynes, *The General Theory of Employment, Interest and Money*, London: Macmillan, 1936, reprinted in D. Moggridge (ed.), *The Collected Writings of John Maynard Keynes*, London: Macmillan, 1971–89, VII, p. 155.
5 M. Magatti, *Libertà Immaginaria*, Milan: Feltrinelli, 2009.

Chapter 1 Why Can We Find No Exit from the Crisis?

1 J. M. Keynes, *The General Theory of Employment, Interest and Money*, London: Macmillan, 1936, reprinted in D. Moggridge (ed.), *The Collected Writings of John Maynard Keynes*, London: Macmillan, 1971–89, VII, p. 162.
2 M. Amato and L. Fantacci, *The End of Finance*, Cambridge: Polity Press, 2011.

3 Cf. ibid., pp. 91–100.
4 J. M. Keynes, 'The General Theory of Employment', *The Quarterly Journal of Economics*, February 1937, *Collected Writings* XIV, p. 116.
5 J. M. Keynes, 'Activities 1940–1944: Shaping the Postwar World, The Clearing Union', *Collected Writings* XXV, pp. 276–7.
6 'Crise bancaire. Le casse du siècle', *Manière de voir. Le Monde diplomatique*, October–November 2011, p. 119.

Chapter 2 The Global Crisis and the Need to Reform the International Monetary and Financial System

1 T. A. Canova, 'Financial Market Failure as a Crisis in the Rule of Law: From Market Fundamentalism to a New Keynesian Regulatory Model', *Harvard Law & Policy Review* III, 2009, pp. 369–96.
2 T. A. Canova, 'Financial Liberalization, International Monetary Dis/Order, and the Neoliberal State', *American University International Law Review* 15(6) (2000): 1279–1319.
3 Federal Reserve press release of 20 October 1987, quoted in M. Carlson, *A Brief History of the 1987 Stock Market Crash with a Discussion of the Federal Reserve Response*, in Finance and Economics Discussion Series, Divisions of Research & Statistics and Monetary Affairs, Federal Reserve Board, Washington, DC, 2007.
4 G. Carli, 'Il disordine nel tempio della finanza internazionale', *Pensieri di un ex governatore*, Pordenone: Edizioni Studio Tesi, 1988, p. 162.
5 Much the same idea was also argued by Ha-Joon Chang, *23 Things They Don't Tell You About Capitalism*, London: Allen Lane, 2010, Thing 22: 'Financial Markets Need to Become Less, Not More, Efficient'.
6 Keynes, *General Theory*, p. 159.
7 *European Commission, Proposal for a Council Directive on a Common System of Financial Transaction Tax and Amending Directive 2008/7/EC*, Brussels, 28 September 2011, COM(2011) 594 final, article 8, p. 19.
8 K. Polanyi, *The Great Transformation*, New York and Toronto: Farrar & Rinehart, 1944.

9 J. A. Schumpeter, *The Theory of Economic Development: An Inquiry into Profits, Capital, Credit, Interest, and the Business Cycle*, Cambridge, MA: Harvard University Press, 1934.

10 'A Deft Way to Buy Time', *Financial Times*, 8 February 2012.

11 See G. Tily, 'Keynes's Theory of Liquidity Preference and His Debt Management and Monetary Policies', *Cambridge Journal of Economics* 30(5) (2006): 657–70.

12 Letter by M. Norman to J. M. Keynes, 20 May 1930, *Collected Writings* XX, p. 349.

13 J. M. Keynes, 'A Drastic Remedy for Unemployment: Reply to Critics', *The Nation and Athenaeum*, 7 June 1924, *Collected Writings* XIX, p. 228.

14 Letter by J. M. Keynes to M. Norman, 22 May 1930, *Collected Writings* XIX, pp. 354–5.

15 J. M. Keynes, *General Theory*, p. 158.

16 'Top Banks in EU Rush for Safety', *Wall Street Journal*, 21 February 2012.

17 When we wrote this proposal in the original Italian version of this book, in the spring of 2012, it sounded so extreme that a student of ours, commenting on a draft of the text, accused us of being naive. One year later, a similar measure is being taken seriously by the governor of the ECB, Mario Draghi.

18 K. Mettenheim, 'Back to Basics in Banking Theory and Varieties of Finance Capitalism', *Accounting, Economics and Law* 3(3): 357–405. Available at http://dx.doi.org/10.1515/ael-2013-0008, May 2013. See also J. Birchall, *Finance in an Age of Austerity: The Power of Customer-Owned Banks*, Cheltenham: Edward Elgar, 2013.

19 F. Morin, *A World Without Wall Street*, Chicago: University of Chicago Press, 2013.

20 'Standing Accused: A Pillar of Finance and Charity', *New York Times*, 13 December 2008.

21 'All Just One Big Lie', *Washington Post*, 13 December 2008.

22 'Fees, Even Returns and Auditor All Raised Flags', *Wall Street Journal*, 13 December 2008.

23 Ibid.

24 Ibid.

25 'Madoff's Auditor … Doesn't Audit?', *Fortune*, 19 December 2008.

26 'Charities: The Foundation of Madoff's Scheme?', available at http://money.cnn.com/2008/12/29/news/newsmakers/zuckoff _madoff.fortune/, last accessed 6 February 2014.

27 'The Affinity Ponzi Scheme', *Newsweek* CLIII(2) (12 January 2009): 39. Available at www.newsweek.com/affinity-ponzi-scheme-78313, last accessed 6 February 2014.

28 'Ex-Nasdaq Chair Arrested on Fraud Charge in NYC', Associated Press, 11 December 2008.

29 'Madoff Chasers Dug for Years, to No Avail', *The Wall Street Journal*, 5 January 2009.

30 'All Just One Big Lie', *Washington Post*, 13 December 2008.

31 'Madoff Exposes Double Standard for Ponzi Schemes', available at Bloomberg.com, last accessed 18 December 2008.

32 Ibid.

33 Speech by SEC Chairman: *Address to Joint Meeting of the Exchequer Club and Women in Housing and Finance by Chairman Christopher Cox*, US Securities and Exchange Commission, Mayflower Hotel, Washington, DC, 4 December 2008.

34 'Fees, Even Returns and Auditor All Raised Flags', *The Wall Street Journal*, 13 December 2008.

35 'Low Rates See Banks Turn to Bundled Mortgage Products', *Financial Times*, 8 February 2012.

36 'US Bank Loans: Battling Back from the Recession as Growth Remains Weak', Standard&Poor, 8 February 2012.

37 'Hordes of Hoarders', *Financial Times*, 30 January 2012.

38 'European Company Defaults Expected to Surge', *Financial Times*, 7 February 2012.

39 Interview with M. Mucchetti, *Corriere della Sera*, 24 February 2012.

40 Letter by J. M. Keynes to M. Norman, 22 May 1930, *Collected Writings* XX, pp. 350–1.

41 J. M. Keynes, *The Economics Prospects 1932*, *Collected Writings* XXI, pp. 39–40.

42 R. Koo, 'The World in Balance Sheet Recession: Causes, Cure, and Politics', *Real-World Economics Review* 58 (12 December 2011): 19–37. Available at www.paecon.net/PAEReview/issue58/Koo58.pdf, last accessed 6 February 2014.

43 Bourse Consult, *London: A Centre for Renminbi Business, City of London Renmimbi Series*, London: City of London Corporation, April 2012, pp. 9–11.

44 'London Goes After Yuan Trading', *Wall Street Journal*, 18 April 2012.

45 Bourse Consult, *London: A Centre for Renminbi Business*, p. 1.

46 'London Goes After Yuan Trading', *Wall Street Journal*, 18 April 2012.

47 City of London, *City Launches New Initiative to Strengthen London's Position as the Leading Western Hub for International RMB Business*, Press Release, 18 April 2012.

48 Ibid.

49 J. M. Keynes, *Eutopia. Proposte per una moneta internazionale*, Milan: Et Al. Edizioni, 2011. A synthesis of the main arguments may be found in 'Why Not Bancor? Keynes's Currency Plan as a Solution to Global Imbalances', in M. C. Marcuzzo, P. Mehrling and T. Hirai (eds), *Keynesian Reflections: Effective Demand, Money, Finance and Policies*, Oxford: Oxford University Press, 2013.

Chapter 3 The European Crisis and the Need for a New European Payments Union

1 Friedrich Hölderlin, *Hyperion and Selected Poems*, ed. Eric L. Santner, The German Library, 22, New York: Continuum, 1990.

2 See also B. Spinelli, 'La perdita dell'olfatto', *la Repubblica*, 18 April 2012.

3 'The Fiscal Treaty that Could Trigger a Debt Explosion', *Financial Times*, 30 January 2012.

4 Official at ECB, 'Hints at Fresh Bond Move', *Financial Times*, 12 April 2012.

5 Cf., on this point, Y. Biondi and L. Fantacci, 'Les banques sont-elles solubles dans le marché? À propos de la comptabilisation de la dette grecque à sa *juste valeur*', *Economies et Sociétés*, s. K, III(2), 2012: 571–84.

6 As we demonstrated in *The End of Finance*, tracing the story back to the invention of that model with the so-called English financial revolution at the end of the seventeenth century.

7 European Commission, 'Widening Current Account Differences within the Euro Area', *Quarterly Report on the Euro Area*, December 2006, p. 32.

8 On this aspect, see also the recent contribution by N. Ferguson and N. Roubini, 'Berlin is Ignoring the Lessons of the 1930s', *Financial Times*, 10 June 2012.

9 A similar proposal was advanced by two members of the German parliament but failed, even in Germany, to arouse the interest it merited. See L. Paus A. Troost, *Eine Europäische Ausgleichsunion. Die Währungsunion 2.0*, Schriftenreihe Denkanstöße, Institut Solidarische Moderne, March 2011 (English and French translations available at www.axel-troost .de/article/5211.eine-europaeische-ausgleichsunion-a-8211 -die-waehrungsunion-2-0.html, last accessed 7 February 2014).

10 P. Spahn, 'Why Exchange Rate Systems Collapse', in T. Hirai, C. Marcuzzo and P. Mehrling (eds), *Keynesian Reflections*, Oxford: Oxford University Press, 2013.

11 Explicit mention is merited at least by the exemplary case of the WIR cooperative bank (www.wir.ch) in Switzerland, which for eighty years has been offering a clearing system denominated in the local currency and, in Italy, the recent but promising Sardex project (www.sardex.net).

12 See, in particular: L. Fantacci, *La moneta. Storia di un'istituzione mancata*, Venice: Marsilio, 2005, 'Monete diverse per usi diversi'; M. Amato, *L'enigma della moneta e l'inizio dell'economia*, Milan: Et Al. Edizioni, 2010, 'Che cos'è propriamente locale nella moneta'.

Chapter 4 Local Currencies and Local Finance

1 On the capacity of complementary currencies founded on the clearing principle to answer the needs of commodity production and trade while avoiding the opposite excesses of inflation and deflation, see the work of Geminello Alvi, in particular *Il capitalismo. Verso l'ideale cinese*, Venice: Marsilio, 2011, pp. 290, 302–5, as well as the authors cited there.

2 A recent report lists more than seven hundred in various parts of the world: City of London Corporation, *Capacity Trade and Credit: Emerging Architectures for Commerce and Money*, December 2011.

3 Cf. on this point Amato, *L'enigma della moneta e l'inizio dell'economia*, in particular pp. 183–239.

4 J. M. Keynes, *A Tract on Monetary Reform*, Collected Writings IV, p. 124.
5 J. M. Keynes, *Collected Writings*, XXV, p. 33.
6 On the distinction between rationality and reasonableness in Keynes, see M. C. Marcuzzo, 'Reason and Reasonableness in Keynes: Rereading *The Economic Consequences of the Peace*', in A. Arnon, J. Weinblatt and W. Young (eds), *Perspectives on Keynesian Economics*, Heidelberg: Springer, 2010, pp. 35–52.

Index